ENGAGING

the

REVELATORY REALM

of

HEAVEN

Previously published *Engaging the Revelatory Realm of Heaven: Entrance to Hidden Mysteries* by Streams Publications copyright 2003
ISBN: 1-58483-085-9

DESTINY IMAGE® PUBLISHERS, INC.

P.O. Box 310, Shippensburg, PA 17257-0310

"Speaking to the Purposes of God for This Generation and for the Generations to Come."

This book and all other Destiny Image, Revival Press, MercyPlace, Fresh Bread, Destiny Image Fiction, and Treasure House books are available at Christian bookstores and distributors worldwide.

For a U.S. bookstore nearest you, call 1-800-722-6774.

For more information on foreign distributors, call 717-532-3040.

Reach us on the Internet: www.destinyimage.com.

ISBN 10:   0-7684-3195-6
ISBN 13:   978-0-7684-3195-7

For Worldwide Distribution, Printed in the U.S.A.

2 3 4 5 6 7 8 9 10 / 18 17 16 15 14

ENGAGING
the
REVELATORY REALM
of
HEAVEN

PAUL KEITH DAVIS

To the saints who have gone before us,
who were the first fruits of God's great
unfolding for all generations.

Contents

INTRODUCTION. 9

CHAPTER 1
Spiritual Beneficiaries .17

CHAPTER 2
A Divine Affirmation .31

CHAPTER 3
A Missed Opportunity 41

CHAPTER 4
Restoration of Our Birthright 53

CHAPTER 5
Living in a Prophetic Generation 75

CHAPTER 6
Attributes of Third Heaven Revelation 93

CHAPTER 7
Equipping Warriors 105

CHAPTER 8
Discerning Spiritual Revelation 115

CHAPTER 9
To Fill the Earth With His Glory 137

CHAPTER 10
Our Prophetic Mandates 147

CHAPTER 11
Tasting the Good Word of God 165

CHAPTER 12
Spiritual Thoughts and Spiritual Words 179

SUMMARY 191

Introduction

In our day of destiny, we will see the glory of God. But in order to see, we must believe.

> *"Jesus said to her, **'Did I not say to you that if you believe, you will see the glory of God?'"*** (John 11:40)

No one could have anticipated Jesus' strategy as He tarried before proceeding to Bethany and raising Lazarus from the dead. That was an unprecedented display of His power and authority. It stretched the faith of Mary and Martha and prepared their eyes to behold God's glory.

Fresh and exceptional things are about to take place in the Church around the world. These things will stretch our faith and uniquely prepare us for an awesome demonstration of God's glory. The Bible fore-tells that the spirit of this generation will be as it was during the days of Noah. The Scriptures portray Noah as one who found favor in God's sight.

Through a divine visitation, God specifically pre-pared Noah for unprecedented events that unfolded in his generation. No human reasoning or natural wisdom could have provided the necessary insight and strategic blueprint for survival. Noah prevailed only by the Spirit of Revelation and obedience to the spoken Word of the Lord.

Only in the supernatural realm can we receive the provision for our generation. This spiritual reality requires a far greater faith than we presently possess on a corporate level. Therefore, we must set our faith in order to access God's end-time promises to the Church. Jesus is the Resurrection and the Life, and He desires to display His resurrection power and life, so we may behold God's glory.

Many aspects of His divine life have not yet been discovered. The God-empowered life is wholly super-natural. It is profoundly prophetic and embodies unfathomable depths of wisdom and knowledge. The prophets and patriarchs of old foresaw the promises given to the end-time generation; they longed to see this manifestation of God's glory on the earth. They foresaw God's plan and marveled at the resources of Heaven reserved for this coming appointment with destiny.

As expressions of God's grace, windows and doors of opportunity will be granted to many of us, granting access to the supernatural dimension of faith. For many decades, we have implemented our various programs and organizational strategies to evangelize the world. Although we are thankful for all who have been touched by this means, it has not produced the bountiful harvest foretold and described in the Scriptures. Strictly by the demonstration of the Holy Spirit and His power will such a harvest be realized!

As we stand on the threshold of the new millennium and the dawning of a new day for the Church, we would be well served to examine our heritage and comprehend more clearly our future. Many Scriptures outline the pattern by which the Lord established His apostolic Church. However, the Book of Hebrews records some characteristics of God's Kingdom:

> *God also testifying with them, both by signs and wonders and by various miracles and by gifts of the Holy Spirit according to His own will* (Hebrews 2:4).

In reality, this passage is forthright and underscores the cooperation between Heaven and earth in presenting the Gospel. Such pointed language as this requires no interpretation, only our faith to believe it. To attempt to explain away this supernatural dimension of our heritage would provide a refuge for cold formal religion and a hiding place for unbelief.

Examining Jesus' commission to bring light to this dark world and to evangelize the nations leaves little room for doubt that the supernatural realms of Heaven are essential in accomplishing His divine mandate. The overall superior strength and abilities of many in the world leave most in the Church feeling inadequate when it comes to natural capabilities and proficiency. However, when united with the assistance of Heaven and the impartation of the supernatural dimension, we can confidently press ahead, generously equipped for the rich demands placed on participants in the end-time army Scripture indicates that God chooses to transform base and common things to confound the wise. Our confidence cannot be drawn from our own strength, but from His.

In no way does this imply an endorsement of ignorance or a lack of excellence. Quite the contrary, God does not intend that we approach the world on its own terms. Our standard is a representation of Heaven according to the perfect model established by Jesus and emulated by the early apostles. Like the apostle Paul, our Gospel cannot rest on superiority of speech and human wisdom but rather, by demonstration of the Spirit and His supernatural power.

Those who approach this Great Commission without the undergirding of true supernatural power and authority from Heaven will most likely return without lasting fruit. For it is Christ in us who is the hope of glory and the fulfillment of the assignment placed upon this unique generation. We cannot approach impossible tasks without being equipped by the God of the impossible. Through Him, we can boldly proclaim that all things are possible. Our only opportunity for victory is to be clothed with Christ and make no provision for the flesh or for human arguments that would deny the power of Heaven.

Many of us have endured much anguish and hardship during our sanctification process that prepares us to share in the harvest and walk in union with God. Great value exists in understanding the purpose for seasons of oppression and privation—they assist in the lofty endeavor of discovering God's rest and experiencing supernatural faith in God's Son. The refining process has as its goal the perfecting of our faith.

It is also through experiencing various trials that we discover the fullness and magnitude of our own weaknesses as well as our great dependency on Him— Christ in us, our hope of glory.

Any form of self-reliance ultimately works counter to the higher purpose of God.

Around the earth today, the Holy Spirit is releasing fresh dimensions of enlightenment regarding His Word, His desires, and His strategies. They are for a mature body of believers to access and disseminate, allowing them to operate more fully in the power and revelatory realms of Heaven. Throughout history, when God's people walked before Him in truthfulness and faithfulness, He made known His presence through visible signs, visions, and displays of His might. A reverential fear of the Lord arises from such demonstrations of God's virtue. That is the quest for this generation.

Presently, an opportunity exists for our spiritual eyes and ears to be illumined, thereby birthing truthful and faithful hearts. A.W. Tozer once expressed it:

> My thoughts aren't adequate, Lord, to enable me to lead Your people through the quagmire of today's society. Nor are

the thoughts of the writers, the teachers, the preachers, and the psychologists
that bombard me from the pages and the
airways. I'm only going to be effective as
a spiritual leader as I learn to think God's
thoughts.[1]

Scripture instructs us that where there is no vision,
people perish. Discouragement and unbelief—resulting
from deferred hope and seemingly unfulfilled promises—will be overcome as the Church apprehends the
revelatory realm of Heaven and secures the thoughts
and ways of God. That is our biblical promise and
spiritual mandate for our generation.

ENDNOTE

1.   A.W. Tozer, *Tozer on Christian Leadership* (Camp
Hill, PA: Wingspread Publishers, 2007).

Chapter 1

SPIRITUAL BENEFICIARIES

One of the most exciting aspects of living in a prophetic generation is the way the Scriptures come to life through the Holy Spirit's anointing imparted through divine encounters with Him. We are living in a time that was foreseen and described by numerous prophets and spiritual forerunners.

According to the Book of Hebrews, many partakers of the heavenly calling longed for this generation and its glorious promise. Although these men and women won divine approval and obtained a powerful testimony, they were not permitted to see the fulfillment of God's promises. Instead, God foresaw something greater and ordained that these former saints would not come to spiritual perfection "apart from us" (see Heb. 11:39-40). Even now, the prayers and sacrifices of these forerunners serve as spiritual seeds of purpose and destiny from which we will derive an inheritance as the spiritual beneficiaries.

Naturally, our redemption and destiny were secured solely through the sacrificial offering of the Lord Jesus and the fulfillment of His promised resurrection. Without His blood and triumph over death, hell, and the grave, there would be no redemptive plan or end-time strategy for the unfolding of the Kingdom of Heaven. All who share in eternal life are grafted into Christ's covenant and scheme of victory through His blood. No other way exists to the Father. Jesus is the only mediator between God and humankind.

With that foundation established, a mystery of the Kingdom is highlighted in the Book of Hebrews that unites previous generations of overcomers with the latter-day plan of God. Believers in the Body of Christ are about to receive a much more comprehensive understanding of the "cloud of witnesses" and their function, as depicted in this passage:

> *And all these, having gained approval through their faith, did not receive what was promised, because God had provided something better for us, so that apart from us they would not be made perfect* (Hebrews 11:39-40).

The Bible plainly points out they would not be made perfect apart from us. What an incredible mystery of the Kingdom we see unfolding in this generation! The unique wording in Hebrews 11 conveys that the Lord had something planned for a future generation that consolidated the sacrificial lives and prayers of notable saints and patriarchs with the unfolding of His end-time plan.

A spiritual partnership will exist between the "cloud of witnesses" and the Church of our day. Fruit from prayers, unfulfilled promises, and spiritual sacrifices that were sown during prior generations will be gathered and released to the Church in the grand unfolding of God's consummation.

Many families, including my own, have lost loved ones in recent years. The Holy Spirit is inspiring spiritual discernment that these departed ones—comprising faithful followers of God throughout the centuries as well as those precious to us in the present generation—are "first fruits." While this is sometimes a difficult truth to embrace when we have lost those who are dear to us, it is also a great source of comfort to know there will be a bountiful spiritual harvest because of their sacrifice and God's grace.

THE CLOUD OF WITNESSES

Jesus identified Himself as a spiritual grain of wheat, which, having perished, will produce a bountiful harvest of wheat like the original grain (see John 12:24). He has also applied that same spiritual principle to the saints who obtained a testimony of approval from Him through the ages. Many of these loved ones are as grains of wheat, who, having perished, will bring forth multiplied grains of wheat in a fruitful harvest. Their deposit was the life of God imparted and entrusted to them, which they carried in their generation.

For four centuries the Israelites labored long and hard in Egypt under the most harsh and abusive conditions imaginable. For many generations, their slave labor empowered Egypt to prosper as the most dominant nation on the face of the earth in that day.

However, when the time came for their liberation, one generation became the beneficiary of 400 years of enforced labor.

God's justice exacted Israel's departure from Egypt with full compensation for their 400 years of sacrifice and labor. The Lord promised that He:

> ...will also judge the nation whom they will serve; and afterward they will come out with many possessions (Genesis 15:14).

The generation of destiny that saw the fulfillment of the prophetic promise for deliverance also became the recipient of the vast wealth accompanying their liberation. Those living in that day became the beneficiaries of the sacrifice, prayers, and innocent blood shed from the time of Israel's captivity to the day of their promised freedom.

AN UNPRECEDENTED GRACE

We are living in a day of unprecedented demonstrations of grace and power from Heaven. We will actually be the heirs and recipients of untold spiritual benefits generated in response to the sacrificial lives of saints throughout the centuries, whose lives were poured out as a drink offering before the Lord. Their example serves as our pattern to touch God's heart and participate with Him in this notable hour.

The Lord Jesus is our ultimate example, and throughout history we discover the witnesses of those who followed in His footsteps. All their prayers to see the promises fulfilled will be fully answered because it was the Holy Spirit making petition through them. Every ounce of innocent blood shed by saints and martyrs will be vindicated through the justice of God, because their lives were demanded in response to the testimony of Jesus Christ in them. It is all about Him.

For many centuries, the enemy has seemingly plundered the Lord's camp. However, God's all-seeing eye has taken note of every gift, anointing, and commission stolen from the Church. God will reinstate them, in their fullness, before the end of the age. He has promised that He would restore all that has been devoured by our adversary. God's system of justice will demand it.

The time has come for God's people to plunder the enemy's camp and reclaim our desolate heritages. According to the pattern of Israel during the day of their exodus,

...the Lord had given the people favor in the sight of the Egyptians, so that they let them have their request. Thus they plundered the Egyptians (Exodus 12:36).

Although many of God's servants could see the promise prophetically and had won divine approval by their faith, they did not fully realize the promise during their lifetime. Yet, Scripture points out that God saw a grander picture and had something better in mind. The writer of Hebrews clearly emphasizes that those devoted saints would not come to perfection apart from us. The Body of Christ is surrounded and encompassed by a great cloud of witnesses who testify of God's faithfulness.

Therefore, since we have so great a cloud of witnesses surrounding us, let us also lay aside every encumbrance, and the sin which so easily entangles us, and let us run with endurance the race that is set before us, fixing our eyes on Jesus, the author and perfecter of faith, who for the joy set before Him endured the cross, despising the shame, and has sat down

at the right hand of the throne of God
(Hebrews 12:1-2).

We, in the end-time generation, have been
bestowed with the great gift of inheriting the
promises. Our forbearer's prayers and sacrifice
are co-joined with ours in the unveiling of God's
grand finale.

All the innocent blood and reservoirs of prayer
harnessed in Heaven will be merged with the intercession and sacrifice of the Lord Himself...captured in a
censer containing a coal from the altar of Heaven and
released back to the earth (see Rev. 8:3-5). Our loved
ones, seemingly taken prematurely or at the height of
their anointing, will witness and share in the fruit of
this intergenerational collaboration.

Much has been invested for this day. A righteous
generation of Christians is preparing to emerge—
clothed in garments of salvation and righteousness
carrying substantial spiritual authority—who will
begin to inherit the promises foreseen for millennia.
God has imparted spiritual eyes that see and ears that
hear, along with a heart of comprehension into God's
mysteries to this end-time company.

We are living at the dawn of a new day that will introduce a much broader understanding of key Scriptures related to our end-time mandate. We will also discover greater dimensions contained in the spiritual realm in which we are seated.

As God's creation, we are both natural and spiritual beings; we function in both the natural and spiritual realms. So the more spiritually minded we become, the greater our apprehension will be of the spiritual domain and its attributes. As we mature in God, we will have an even greater awareness of the economy of Heaven and the wonderful mysteries hidden in that realm. God will grant a special anointing for *eyes and ears* to envision His promises and comprehend their significance.

It is humbling to contemplate that our forefathers, who lived lives of devotion and sacrifice, never had the opportunity to participate in the prophetic destiny they foresaw. Nevertheless, their prayers and the innocent blood they shed will be remembered as the "books" are opened and the Lord acknowledges their labor on His behalf and releases "compensation" to our generation.

THE END OF TIME

The prophet Daniel recognized this generation and described it as the "time of the end," in which knowledge will increase and great mysteries of the Kingdom will be revealed (see Dan. 12:4). Many believers are entreating the Lord to show great and mighty (hidden and set apart) things we presently do not know.

The prophet Jeremiah was given the following promise when he spoke on behalf of the Lord:

> *Call to Me and I will answer you, and I will tell you great and mighty things, which you do not know* (Jeremiah 33:3).

If we are instructed earnestly to call upon the Lord, then its clear implication is that we will be endowed with the ability to hear from Him with precision and clarity! In this way, we will understand the articulation of prominent and awesome things that we presently do not know. It will be the unveiling of divine truth and the blueprint of Heaven for our time.

OUR SOURCE OF TRUTH

In our quest to understand truth, we can turn to only one source as our absolute standard by which all truth is weighed—the Word of God. The revealed truth—gleaned from the merger of the Word and the Spirit—provides all that we need in this life and the one to come. Through redemption, the covenant promises and blessings are made available to us, as well as the unveiling of the nature and character of God.

The Scriptures and the spiritual impartation they convey are the only pattern by which we may know with certainty the events and directions of the future. They are the only source that satisfactorily answers the questions: Where did I come from? Why am I here? Where am I going?

As someone once said, "Time can take nothing from the Bible. It is the living monitor. Like the sun, it is the same in its life and influence to humanity this day as it was years ago. It can meet every present inquiry and console every present loss."

Resident within the heart of spirit-filled believers should inherently be a great love for the Scriptures and for the truth they convey. It is the sword that separates spirit from soul—light from darkness. Although we are eternally grateful for the understanding we now have, deep wells of spiritual insight, mysteries, and truth remain to be discovered.

VAST OCEANS OF TRUTH

Perhaps many today can understand Sir Isaac Newton's perceptions when he wrote:

> I do not know what I may appear to the world, but to myself I seem to have been only like a boy playing on the seashore and diverting myself in now and then finding a smoother pebble or a prettier shell than ordinary, whilst the great ocean of truth lay all undiscovered before me.[1]

An ocean of divine truth exists before us to be discovered by those anointed with the Spirit of Wisdom and Revelation. Ephesians 1:17-18 emphasizes the right of every believer to be anointed with the Spirit of Wisdom and Revelation. This wisdom is not merely the ability to mentally analyze a situation and make a good response. Rather, it is a spiritual endowment that allows a believer to explore deep into the heart of the Father, to perceive and understand the mysteries of the Kingdom and one's rights purchased through Christ's redemption.

Not only do we have the liberty to understand vast spiritual mysteries, but also the accompanying spirit of Revelation to give illumination and comprehension of their reality. By them we may know...

1. What is the hope of His calling…
   (Eph. 1:18).

2. What are the riches of the glory of
   His inheritance in the saints…
   (Eph. 1:18).

3. What is the surpassing greatness of
   His power toward us who believe…
   (Eph. 1:19).

But there must be an anointing resting upon our spiritual eyes that we may see and our ears that we may hear—anointed eyes and ears. Currently, we have a very limited understanding of the rich deposit of truth inherent in the Scriptures. Part of our mandate during this time in history is to unfold and demonstrate great redemptive truths as part of the hidden manna set apart and reserved for the end-time generation. Those with spiritual comprehension will have great insight and shine brilliantly in this dark age.

ENDNOTE

1. http://thinkexist.com/quotes/isaac_newton/

Chapter 2

A DIVINE
AFFIRMATION

In November 2002, Bob Jones, Bobby Connor, and I were conducting a conference in Albany, Oregon. On the first morning, while we were praying before our pre-conference breakfast, the Holy Spirit released a series of Scriptures to me clearly expressing the motif "eyes and ears." About seven Scriptures flowed in succession, each emphasizing the importance of our eyes and ears being anointed to perceive our covenant blessings. Each truth contributed essential understanding necessary to participate with the Lord in His plan for this season in history. I wrote the Scriptures in my journal, along with notations of what I heard.

As I proceeded to breakfast and entered the meeting room, Bob Jones began to share a penetrating prophetic experience given to him that morning by the Holy Spirit. This is not an unusual occurrence for Bob; he normally receives revelation associated with our meetings and conferences. However, this experience seemed especially meaningful, both in its content and the manner in which the revelation was given.

A HEAVENLY MESSENGER

In the spiritual vision, Bob encountered a heavenly being who brought to our team a message of preparation—not just for that conference but for the Church's present spiritual season. The experience was very similar to one given to the apostle John and recorded in the Bible. The Scriptures portray the aged apostle as receiving insight from a heavenly messenger who admonished and corrected John saying:

> *I am a fellow servant of yours and of your brethren the prophets and of those who*

heed the words of this book. Worship God (Revelation 22:9).

The Lord continues to follow this biblical pattern of releasing messengers with supernatural insight who visit us with expressions of His heart and His mind.

The messenger who came to Bob at the inauguration of this conference in Oregon had a distinguished countenance—he conveyed both authority and humility. Bob Jones, Bobby Connor, and I believe his appearance in itself conveyed an important message. True spiritual influence with both God and humanity is equated with broken and contrite hearts that are fully yielded to God.

During this supernatural encounter, specific instructions were given to those within the Body of Christ yearning to witness the restoring of organs, lame limbs, and other creative miracles. The heavenly messenger emphasized that these signs and wonders will begin to be demonstrated when "unity among the brethren" becomes reality (see Ps. 133). Unity is a more important issue to the Lord than most believers realize. If the Lord can find just a few who are willing to lay down their lives, plans, agendas, and ministries for their brothers and sisters, He will transform cities and regions. This is not to be confused with a pseudo form of counterfeit unity that will also permeate our present age. Rather, it is one that this generation must aspire to be birthed in genuine love and fraternal affection among those bound by a commitment to love the Lord wholly.

Clearly, the Lord is not deceived by our idolatrous attempts to create something from our own mind or image. The apostle Paul demonstrated this willingness to lay down his life as a living sacrifice for the people with whom and to whom he ministered.

> *For I am afraid that perhaps when I come I may find you to be not what I wish and may be found by you to be not what you wish; that perhaps there will be strife, jealousy, angry tempers, disputes, slanders, gossip, arrogance, disturbances* (2 Corinthians 12:20).

The heavenly messenger pointed out that ambition among believers opens the door for suspicion; suspicion brings competition; and competition breeds division. When suspicion and competition are present, it will motivate leaders to discredit or undermine other leaders they feel threatened by.

This kind of spirit cannot exist in the hearts of those to whom the Lord desires to release substantial spiritual power and authority. It will actually disqualify some, if it is not properly dealt with and submitted to the grace of God and the work of His Spirit.

Our ministry team has continued to receive the affirming word that prophetic mandates are being released for cities such as Mobile, Alabama, and regions. The way ministries with prophetic mandates do ministry will be substantially changed in the coming days. The emphasis will become centered on a regional message, not simply a message for one church or another. It will be as it was when the apostle John was caught up to Heaven and received divine messages for the Body of believers living in the seven regions of Asia.

BEAUTIFUL TO THE EYES AND EARS

While the message about unity was prominent in this visitation, other aspects of the visitation were the most encouraging and are those we are thoroughly pursuing. As the messenger was about to depart, he told Bob that I would have understanding of who he (the messenger) was and to have me determine the meaning of his name—Sundar. Naturally, no one in the meeting knew the definition of this name.

Upon returning to my room, I began the search for the meaning of *Sundar*. To my surprise, I discovered its meaning in a dictionary of Indian names as "beautiful, handsome, pleasant to the eyes and ears." What an incredible affirmation of the revelation that came before our breakfast meeting. This stressed the excellence of a fresh anointing and blessing for those prepared to have their *eyes and ears* opened to Kingdom truth and the unfolding of God's mysteries.

SON OF MAN—MARK WELL

The first Scripture that came that morning was Ezekiel 44:4-5. This passage exhorts the prophet to *see with his eyes and hear with his ears* all that was about to be conveyed to him. The pronouncement of this admonition not only conveys the importance of seeing and hearing, but also releases the spiritual impartation necessary to do so.

> *Then He brought me by way of the north gate to the front of the house; and I looked, and behold, the glory of the Lord filled the house of the Lord, and I fell on my face.*

The Lord said to me, "Son of man, mark well, see with your eyes and hear with your ears all that I say to you concerning all the statutes of the house of the Lord and concerning all its laws; and mark well the entrance of the house, with all exits of the sanctuary" (Ezekiel 44:4-5).

Ezekiel was instructed to "mark well." This expression is sometimes translated "set your heart" to understand (see Ezek. 44:5 AMP). There is something inherently connected with *eyes and ears* being opened that allows the heart to comprehend.

The prophet discovered that there is an important aspect to the discernment of the heart that is readily merited by eyes that see and ears that hear instruction from the Lord concerning statutes and ordinances involving His house. As the Scriptures point out, God is building a spiritual house, and the Holy Spirit is providing the essential "blueprint" for its design. Those used in this building program will possess humble and contrite hearts and tremble at God's Word. They will have eyes that see and ears that hear.

The mantle of revelation and power that rested on Ezekiel in his office as a prophet yielded the necessary spiritual tools required to stand as the Lord's representative on earth. The awakening of Ezekiel's "eyes and ears" provided an open door to the realm of the Spirit and an awareness of the thoughts and ways of God for that generation. To be the Lord's representation on earth for our day, we likewise must possess that aspect of the Lord's virtue.

Like John, our quest must be "in the Spirit" on the Lord's day and to behold the door of opportunity standing open before us, that we too might see and apprehend the revelation of the Lord on His throne, the panorama of Heaven, and the orchestration of His Kingdom design (see Rev. 1). It is an essential ingredient in the formula of God for His people to be victorious "overcomers" who experientially discover friendship with God.

This will be the poetic fulfillment of the loving portrayal in Song of Solomon, as Jesus emerges from the wilderness with his enchanted bride leaning upon His shoulder, hearing the slightest whisper that proceeds from His lips (see Song of Sol. 8:5).

A clarion call echoes throughout the Church today to mark well and understand in our hearts all that Jesus will convey. Some will see with their eyes and hear with their ears all that Jesus says involving His house. They will mark the way of entrance to qualify as participants in His grand plan; they will mark the "exits" or issues that will disqualify us from the holy partnership with Him in this end-time strategy.

Joshua and Caleb displayed in their hearts an agreement with God and His *thoughts and ways* to obtain the inheritance promised generations before. Unfortunately, many others did not, and it cost them dearly.

Chapter 3

A MISSED
OPPORTUNITY

A fter 40 years of governing Israel's people in
the wilderness, Moses came to the end of his
journey and recorded a fateful discovery that pro-
hibited his generation from entering the Promised
Land. He admonished them by reiterating the great
and awesome deeds and powerful demonstrations
that the Lord had performed in their midst. He also

underscored a sad reality—that generation did not receive the promise because *"to this day the Lord has not given you a heart to know, nor eyes to see, nor ears to hear"* (Deut. 29:4).

What a valuable lesson for us to heed in our day. Although we can witness notable expressions of spiritual power and authority, these things in themselves are not enough. It remains imperative for us to receive an impartation from the Holy Spirit to possess eyes and ears open to His truth with hearts of understanding. Without that spiritual endowment, we cannot enter the fullness of the promise. Not only do we have an inheritance in Him, but He also has an inheritance in us. Our spiritual eyes and ears must be expanded to facilitate that union.

The truest form of spiritual comprehension requires the Holy Spirit, through the grace of God, to impart the Spirit of Revelation. Those contending for and receiving this grace will begin to see with their eyes, hear with their ears, and comprehend in their hearts the unveiling of God's plan and ascertain willingness to participate in it. Apart from the Spirit of Revelation, spiritual dullness will prevail, as has been historically demonstrated.

Nonetheless, we cannot point a condemning finger at our ancestors. Isolated from this grace, we would also abort the birthing of God's purposes in our generation. Ideally, reexamining the reproof given to the generation typifying ours, will stimulate us to radically pursue and embrace having our hearts filled with desire for intimacy with the Lover of our soul and with the passion to possess illumined spiritual eyes and ears.

DISCOVERING THE PROMISED LAND

The apostle Paul once prayed that our eyes would be illumined with spiritual understanding (see Eph. 1:18). He continually gave thanks and made mention of the Ephesian church, hoping they might possess the ability to discover their rich inheritance in Christ by awakening to the Spirit of Revelation. During a season of discipline, Jerusalem was chastened with a closure of this realm when the prophet Isaiah said,

> *The Lord has poured over you a spirit of deep sleep, He has shut your eyes, the prophets; and He has covered your heads, the seers. The entire vision will be to you like the words of a sealed book, which when they give it to the one who is literate,*

saying, "Please read this," he will say, "I cannot, for it is sealed" (Isaiah 29:10-11).

It is not the Lord's intent for this generation to remain in a deep sleep. Rather, it is His aspiration to enlighten us with prophetic insight and uncover our heads. He wants governmental leadership endowed with Kingdom authority and power. To prepare us to walk into our destiny, the seal is being broken and great mysteries of the Kingdom are being deposited into the hearts of overcomers.

The Lord has promised once again to deal marvelously with His people. Through the Church, God plans to openly demonstrate that the world's wisdom will perish and the worldly discernment and agendas of this present age will be concealed. God has a higher way, and it will be confided in and expressed through His covenant people.

It is an important spiritual mandate to have enlightened eyes to see where we are currently placed in human history and in the unfolding of God's redemptive plan. It is equally important to have eyes that can see ahead to our prophetic destination. From this enlightened perspective, we can set our gaze on the goal of our faith and recognize the enemy's snares that are intended to hinder us.

O Lord, Open His Eyes

On one unique occasion, the prophet Elisha who had spiritual insight as to where he was and where he was going, boldly stood before the king of Aram's armies. He could do so because of the Spirit of Wisdom and Revelation that rested upon his life. When Elisha's servant nervously recited what his natural eyes were seeing, the prophet prayed:

> *"O Lord, I pray, open his eyes that he may see." And the Lord opened the servant's eyes, and he saw; and behold, the mountain was full of horses and chariots of fire all around Elisha* (2 Kings 6:17).

With that prayer, an impartation of spiritual sight was given to his servant. Through that blessing, the servant saw with spiritual eyes that Heaven's armies and fiery chariots surrounded God's prophet.

With keen spiritual vision, fear is replaced with faith; a comprehension is imparted that there are more for us than for the enemy. Nothing really changed in this scenario except the vision of Elisha's servant. Without question, after seeing with spiritual eyes, his faith level soared. His countenance and courage were not based on what he saw with his natural eyes. His spiritual eyes provided clarity to the entire picture.

The Bible promises that to each believer a measure of faith is given (see Rom. 12:3). However, a much higher realm of faith can be accessed when our eyes and ears are expanded to see and hear the unseen heavenly realm. According to Galatians 2:20, we need to begin walking in faith, realizing that God's Spirit lives within us:

> *I have been crucified with Christ; and it is no longer I who live, but Christ lives in me; and the life which I now live in the flesh I live by faith in the Son of God, who loved me, and gave Himself up for me* (Galatians 2:20).

This dimension of faith can only be discovered in God's supernatural realm. The early apostles knew this reality and did exploits full of God's glory.

In formulating our objectives, the apostle Paul once declared that we are not to consider things that are seen but those that are unseen. Visible things are temporal and fleeting, while spiritual and invisible things are everlasting (see 2 Cor. 4:18).

What an incredible illustration of the importance of making decisions that are not merely based on those things we observe with our natural eyes. We need the anointing of the Holy Spirit to remove the veil from our spiritual eyes, so we may see and comprehend our supernatural provisions. Without the Holy Spirit's anointing, the natural realm will strive to steal our faith and the reality of our birthright.

A PRESENT OPPORTUNITY

One of the most prominent invitations being offered Christians is the admonition to *"come up here"* (see Rev. 4:1). This expression denotes a divine call to proceed through an open door to a heavenly realm that can be accessed in this generation. Throughout history, we have discovered a few individuals who were forerunners to this secret place in God. Many saints journeyed beyond that door and walked with the Lord in profound and supernatural ways. These individuals serve as prototypes of a company of men and women who will characterize the latter days.

At certain times throughout history, this door into the heavenly realm has been opened to those who pressed into the Lord and obtained a favorable testimony from God. Like Jacob, some saw the heavens open and a stairway with heavenly hosts ascending and descending.

It was their privilege to discover significant mysteries of God's Kingdom, in ways similar to that of the apostle Paul. He was esteemed with divine favor and was granted numerous visions, revelations, and appearances of Jesus Christ. Entrance to the third Heaven was granted to him; he saw the unveiling of God's Kingdom before the throne. In our generation, a greater awareness of this dimension will come to those who bring forth their revelation of the Kingdom from God's throne.

THE FRIENDS OF GOD

The Scripture says, *"Abraham believed God, and it was accounted to him for righteousness. And he was called the friend of God"* (James 2:23 NKJV).

What higher privilege and experience could be granted to humankind than to be granted admission into the company of those called God's friends? God first established the forum for divine/human friendships to exist. It would be inexcusably presumptuous for any person to say, "I am a friend of God," unless God had first identified that being His friend was possible. As part of our heritage and spiritual inheritance, we are given this unthinkable privilege that must be pursued and attained through God's grace. Our generation will be remembered as the season of friendship with God because of the numbers of people who will discover that reality.

Numerous pioneers went before us to blaze this spiritual trail. They became acutely conscious of the presence of God. They gave everything to maintain that realization for the remainder of their lives. Men and women like A.W. Tozer, Maria Woodworth-Etter, John G. Lake, William Branham, Alexander Dowie, Walter Beuttler, and many others who perhaps were never known publicly—men and women who tasted union with God and discovered His rest.

Human history records the amazing power for good that God exercised in those who ascended to the experiential reality of friendship with Him. These men and women walked in conscious communion with the tangible presence of God and lived with the mindful conviction that their prayers were expressed to Someone perceivably present. In our day, this alone is our highest aspiration and one that will be attained by many.

AN EXPERIENTIAL REALITY

The Bible stresses that we are positionally seated with Christ in heavenly places (see Eph. 2:6). Once that heritage becomes an experiential certainty, our conscious awareness will be centered in that place of residence, rather than in our natural surroundings. Our decisions and actions will be dictated by the understanding we obtain in the eternal realm. Like Elisha's servant, when our eyes are illumined to the spiritual domain, our perspectives will change.

In our day, a first-fruits demonstration will accompany this reality of those who come to a place of maturity first and function as pioneers for the harvest to follow. Like spies who venture into the Promised Land to discover the grapes of Eshcol, many will taste God's good Word and the supernatural powers of the eternal age to come (see Heb. 6:5). The outcome will be a representation of Kingdom dimension, and authority displayed through humble and contrite vessels. This expression of the Lord's grace will awaken the Body of Christ to her destiny and cause her to abandon all else to pursue Him, the true Pearl of great price.

A joining of the Head to the Body must occur. Jesus is described in the Scriptures as the Head, and His followers are His Body. Through us, He will articulate the Father's thoughts and desires. Unity can only function from a position of compatibility between Jesus and His Body.

Focused concentration is now required on each person's nature and character in order for him or her to experience divine visions and revelations in the manner of the apostles Paul and John. This privilege is offered to every believer. However, grooming and proper equipping is necessary to inhabit these high places in God.

Possessing the desire and desperation to comprehend this reality is a gift from the Holy Spirit. Our earnest prayer should be for the Holy Spirit to "make us ready," without guile or tendencies to corrupt His sacred place. It was once spoken of Nathanael that he was an Israelite in whom there was no guile (see John 1:47 KJV). Our prayer should be for the Lord to make such a proclamation about us and grant an awakening to our eyes and ears.

Chapter 4

RESTORATION OF OUR BIRTHRIGHT

A restoration is taking place involving a believer's understanding of the spiritual birthright and inheritance of God's covenant people. After Adam's transgression, the Bible declares that his eyes were opened and he discovered that he was naked. A transference of vision took place in the Garden. This transference is what the Lord wishes to redeem in us today.

Adam was created with the weighty privilege of seeing the Lord with his eyes and hearing Him with his ears, as he and God walked in the cool of the day. We are now living in the cool-of-the-day or evening-time season. Spiritual sight and sound are being effectually restored, allowing a righteous generation to walk with the Lord in single-mindedness and unity.

We can pursue God's revelatory realm with radical and earnest expectation. We can experience supernatural places in God spoken of in the Scriptures and found in the pages of history that recount the lives of devout saints who became God's friends. Their testimonies point to a deep and abiding fellowship with God and supernatural encounters with the eternal realm.

The Bible records that prior to Adam and Eve's transgression, they were both naked and unashamed (see Gen. 2:25). Transparent before God, they walked with Him without shame or reservation. They saw with their eyes and heard with their ears the Creator of the universe as He walked and talked with them according to His original design.

God yearns to restore the order of redemption—to put back into its original state, to redeem. Originally, Adam was perfectly fashioned with complete and harmonious union of spirit, soul, and body. No conflict was found in his nature. However, after the fall, his soul—like ours—became the battlefield between light and dark (see Rom. 7:14-25).

Through the promise of restoration, we can once again achieve that place of harmony and divine union. We can experience the complete yielding of our will to the Father's will. We can find a place of rest and enjoy open fellowship that Adam previously enjoyed in the Garden of Eden. This is the secret in the life and ministry of Kathryn Kuhlman, who touched this reality in God and transformed her generation.

Through the promise for the restoration, we can set our faith to once again walk with God and hear His intimate expressions. As His children, we have been given the unfathomably rich promise to see the Lord with unveiled faces (see 2 Cor. 3:18). Our eyes and ears can be restored to the place of God's original design, and our hearts can be free from shame.

Inherent in our spiritual heritage, we have the privilege and admonition to know the perpetual, conscious communion with God that is outlined and exemplified in the Scriptures and demonstrated in the lives of a few saints throughout history. We cannot allow the enemy's efforts to succeed in clouding our heritage through unbelief. Plenty of naysayers ardently deny and criticize this aspect of our end-time commission. Nonetheless, a company of people will ascend into the faith realms of Heaven to acquire this dimension of Kingdom certainty.

Revealed by the Spirit

The Holy Spirit, through the apostle Paul, highlighted a profound reality that a coming generation will know in fullness:

> But just as it is written, 'Things which eye has not seen and ear has not heard, and which have not entered the heart of man, all that God has prepared for those who love Him.' For to us God revealed them through the Spirit; for the Spirit searches all things, even the depths of God (1 Corinthians 2:9-10).

Knowing the Spirit of Revelation is essential to our walk so that we claim our rich inheritance in Christ. Even more, that same Spirit is fundamentally necessary to our comprehension that Jesus Christ has a birthright in us. The Levitical priests did not receive an inheritance because the Lord was their inheritance;

they were given the distinguished honor of ministering to the Lord as part of this.

We must understand this great mystery in God that involves us being His inheritance and the body to which the Head must be fashioned. Foreshadowed in the Old Testament, this mystery is the Word becoming flesh and dwelling not just among us but within us.

God has many exciting and extraordinary thoughts and plans for our generation. These are reserved and hidden within His heart and conveyed through His Word. A prophetic *word* is a thought that has been given discernible language. Jesus is actually the purest expression of the *anointed Word*. He is the Word of God incarnate—the Messiah, the Anointed One. He is the perfect articulation of God's thoughts and ways depicted in human form.

We are transported from the natural into the spiritual realm through the anointed Word that functions as a spiritual passage. The anointing of God is essential in this journey. His thoughts and mysteries are apprehended when we are thrust into the Spirit through His anointing.

When a natural word is given, it becomes *spiritual* by the Holy Spirit's anointing (see 2 Cor. 3:6). The Lord said His words were both life and spirit. The Spirit gives life to the message of the Kingdom, pointing to the cross and transporting us from the natural realm into the spiritual realm. It is in that place our eyes and ears are opened and we discover the hope of our calling and the immeasurable greatness of His unlimited power toward those who believe.

According to First Corinthians 2, the Spirit of Revelation grants us access to the mind of Christ and His exceedingly rich portrait of purpose and destiny. By embracing the grace to be equipped with illumined eyes and ears, we are grafted into His scheme of victory when our insight is coupled with a resounding "yes" from our hearts. This dimension of revelation is being given to achieve an ideal agreement between Heaven and earth.

God is combining spiritual thoughts with spiritual words that are both seen and heard. The Spirit of Revelation anoints our eyes and ears, which provides comprehension to our hearts, thereby allowing His thoughts and ways to be imparted to His people. This has been the case in every expression of revival since the days of Martin Luther. The church discovered the things that were important to God through these expressions of revival involving Luther, Wesley, Charles Parham, William J. Seymour, and others who identified the relevant message of God's Kingdom for their generation. Kingdom mandates reserved for this hour cannot be acquired or fully appreciated by mere human wisdom. Our only hope is to be consumed by the Holy Spirit, who furnishes the precise representation of spiritual truth through spiritual language.

Receiving revelation from the Lord on a perpetual basis is not merely a gift. It's part of who we truly are—spiritually minded people who receive their spiritual DNA from the Lord Himself. Through this priestly endowment, all those things our eyes have not seen, our ears have not heard, and our minds have not yet imagined, God is unveiling with a deeper understanding to those who love Him, who hold Him in affectionate reverence, and who recognize His many blessings.

UNDERSTANDING THE KINGDOM MESSAGE

In the Parable of the Sower, Jesus explained His unique teaching and the human condition regarding our acceptance of the Kingdom message:

When anyone hears the word of the kingdom, and does not understand it, the evil one comes and snatches away what has been sown in his heart. This is the one on whom seed was sown beside the road....And the one on whom seed was sown on the good soil, this is the man who hears the word and understands it; who indeed bears fruit and brings forth, some a hundredfold, some sixty, and some thirty (Matthew 13:19,23).

The one upon whom the seed is sown to manifest fruit thirty, sixty, and a hundredfold, is the one who hears the message of the Kingdom and understands it. The one without understanding has the Kingdom seed snatched away and devoured by the fowl of the air. Comprehension—produced by the Spirit of Revelation within a person's heart—is essential in accepting the message and leading to lasting fruitfulness.

In this parable, the word *understanding* denotes a hostile form of combat or repositioning. Thus, to receive comprehension allows for the displacement of one thing and its replacement by something else. In this spiritual transference, confusion is replaced by spiritual insight; hopelessness is overcome by hope; darkness is overwhelmed by light; and fear is displaced by faith.

Jesus blessed His disciples because they were graced with eyes to see and ears to hear (see Matt. 13:16). In a similar way, God is more concerned about what we are becoming than what we are doing. In order to become like Him and a worthy representation of Heaven on earth, we must possess spiritual eyes that see via the revelation unfolding of His divine plan, along with awakened ears to hear the truth of His message. Throughout the ages, many prophets and righteous people desired to see what our eyes will see and hear what our ears will hear. In these days, the Holy Spirit is searching the depths of God's heart and is unveiling the Lord's mind, yearning to release more of God to an overcoming Body that represents His Kingdom.

BEHOLDING OUR TEACHER

Another Scripture that was given that morning in Albany, Oregon, and one that has been a favorite of mine over the years, is taken from the prophet Isaiah:

> O people in Zion, inhabitant in Jerusalem, you will weep no longer. He will surely be gracious to you at the sound of your cry; when He hears it, He will answer you. Although the Lord has given you bread of privation and water of oppression, He, your Teacher will no longer hide Himself, but your eyes will behold your Teacher. Your

ears will hear a word behind you, "This is the way, walk in it," whenever you turn to the right or to the left. And you will defile your graven images overlaid with silver, and your molten images plated with gold. You will scatter them as an impure thing, and say to them, "Be gone!" (Isaiah 30:19-22)

In this prophetic proclamation, Isaiah is pointing to a day of favor and restoration. It will be a day in which the cries of His people are heard and the answer forthcoming.

That day has now arrived. Resident within the hearts of many lovesick Christians is a cry for the restoration of the promise of intimacy with Jesus and the unveiling of His glory. Following this intercessory appeal, the Lord vows to be gracious to us.

Although for a season God has given us the bread of privation and water of oppression, He, our Teacher, will no longer hide Himself from us. Instead, He will make Himself accessible; our eyes will see Him and our ears will hear His words.

Throughout the Body of Christ, there are many hungry hearts longing to encounter the Lord on a personal level. For them, it is not enough to hear reports of others who have profoundly discovered and experienced the Lord. They must have an experiential appointment that will transform their lives and open a door to new realms of the Spirit.

This season of privation and oppression is necessary to sift from our character the corruption of this world and to allow us to walk in this dimension without prostituting or corrupting its purity. For the past several years, those who will see and hear the Teacher have been groomed and prepared for this time. This season's purpose is to groom a people who will become stewards of Heaven's mysteries and creative power.

Through the help of the Holy Spirit, this company of believers will guard the extravagant spiritual treasures entrusted to them; they will not squander their spiritual inheritance. Once achieved in the hearts of His faithful servants, this outpouring of God's Spirit can be sustained because of the meticulous preparation and readiness provided by the Holy Spirit.

DAVID'S EXAMPLE

Although David's destiny was one of greatness and divine favor, he was required to endure persecution and hardship before being released into the fullness of his calling. It was during these difficult years that character was being forged to prepare him for being a king. Decisions he made in the wilderness helped formulate the pattern of David's life when he ascended to the throne.

A similar situation has occurred for many in the Church. It appears our enemies have prevailed over us, despite great promises given to us by the Holy Spirit. However, it is during persecution and hardship that divine character is formed in us; we are purged and purified from our own carnality and equipped to faithfully accommodate the anointing. Righteous decisions that are made during these dry intervals will reap immeasurable dividends throughout the coming seasons of great prosperity.

While experiencing the baptism of trials, it is challenging to wait upon the Lord for His perfect timing in releasing all His promises to us. Like David, we cry out to the Lord, "How long must we endure these difficult and trying times?" Patiently, the Lord admonishes us to "be still" and wait for the completion of His sanctifying work of grace within us, allowing the full release of His anointing through us. However, our tendency during these times is to do something. So we often misinterpret ministry activity as *doing the will of the Father* and confuse endless motion with progress.

In Matthew 7, Jesus describes many who were involved in ministry—healing the sick, casting out devils, performing miracles—but their eternal destiny was outer darkness.

> *Not everyone who says to Me, 'Lord, Lord,' will enter the kingdom of heaven; but he who does the will of My Father who is in heaven...* (Matthew 7:21).

In doing the Father's will, we access the Kingdom of Heaven and find favor and grace during times of need. In the Scripture, one of the Hebrew terms translated as "salvation" is *yeshuash*[1] that denotes deliverance, welfare, prosperity, and victory. Its unique application bespeaks deliverance from present troubles and the assurance that the Lord is aware of our condition and will intervene on our behalf. He assures us, saying:

> *"I know the plans that I have for you," declares the Lord, "plans for welfare and not for calamity to give you a future and a hope"* (Jeremiah 29:11).

Our Savior's plans for us are for welfare and prosperity, not calamity. However, wilderness

experiences are allowed to establish godly character in us and to allow us to sow seeds of righteousness that will reap bountiful harvests in the seasons
ahead. We must pray with the same assurance as
David, despite the external circumstances and trust-
ingly realize that the Lord is faithful to His promises. Not one of His promises has ever failed in all
of history.

Beholding God's Beauty

After years of walking with the Lord, David gave
expression to his heart's longing. He had ultimately
concluded there was only one thing he truly desired
and one thing that would fully satisfy the purpose of
his life: to dwell in the house of the Lord all the days
of his life and to behold the beauty of the Lord and
meditate in His Temple (see Ps. 27:4).

David's passion was to gaze upon and perceive
the Lord's beauty and delight in His loveliness. His
expression signifies an experiential comprehension of
the beauty realm of Heaven.

Can we behold the King in all His beauty? In
Isaiah 33:14-15, the Holy Spirit through the prophet
Isaiah asks a revealing question: "Who can live with
continual burning?" Or, in other words, *Who can live*

in an atmosphere where there are perpetual expressions of God's justice? The prophet provides the answers:

1. The one who walks righteously.

2. The one who speaks with sincerity.

3. The one who rejects unjust gain.

4. The one who shakes his hands so that they hold no bribe.

5. The one who stops his ears from hearing about bloodshed.

6. The one who shuts his eyes from looking upon evil.

Such a person lives in a state of consecration and purity, which allows them to dwell in the heavenly heights; their refuge will be the impregnable Rock. Such a person's heavenly bread will be provided and their spiritual water source will be sure. Such a person's eyes will see the King in all of His beauty and will behold the far-distant land (see Isa. 33:14-17).

Although the Lord first appeared as the suffering Lamb, He is now being revealed as the victorious

King. Heaven is unveiling the Lord's great glory and kingly authority. It is our outstanding privilege to be offered the opportunity to possess anointed eyes to see, behold, and perceive the revelation of the King and His Kingdom.

According to biblical scholars and noted in Vine's Expository Dictionary, the Hebrew word *chazah* means "to see, behold, or select for oneself." It appears 54 times and in every period of biblical Hebrew. *Chazah* literally signifies the ability to see "in a prophetic vision or as a seer in an ecstatic state." In Numbers 24:4 the word means "to see by way of a prophet's vision, to see with intelligence and by an experience."

Through biblical promises, opportunities are given to apprehend experientially the glory attributes of God in perceptible and tangible ways. The sum of David's passions were captured in that one thing—the desire of the Lord. May it also be our chief desire to see, behold, comprehend, and explore the mysteries and infinite riches of the Lord's goodness and beauty.

Just as our five natural senses engage the physical world, so also do our spiritual senses access the spiritual realm. In Scripture, we are admonished to taste and see that the Lord is good. To do so, some spiritual virtue must exist that will allow us passage to that realm in order to savor and to observe God's goodness.

Throughout the Song of Solomon, various oils and fragrances are highlighted as prophetic symbols to portray spiritual reality involving God's nature. An actual fragrance of Heaven can be discerned which often depicts attributes of the Lord's beauty and presence for specific purposes.

Within our spiritual heritage, we are endowed with the means to discover that glorious realm of the Spirit. Through our spiritual faculties, we are able to apprehend the attributes of that domain when the Holy Spirit has awakened those senses. If we remain carnally minded and overcome by unbelief, these spiritual faculties will never achieve the purpose for which they were given. It should be our earnest prayer to possess full access to our spiritual senses—to see, hear, taste, smell, and even touch Kingdom realities that surround us. Spiritual things are spiritually discerned.

To desire to live by the Spirit more than life itself is not a demanding or wearisome thing to the Lord. It greatly pleases Him! That passion will consume His bride and allow her to fully appropriate her spiritual heritage and faithfully consummate her marriage to the Lamb.

SUSTAINING
THE ANOINTING

Throughout history we have witnessed the disheartening brevity of prior expressions of revival and outpouring. The Lord seems to prophetically indicate that He desires to release something that is not short-lived, but long-term and maintained by His people moving from prominent expressions of glory to even more distinguished demonstrations of His glory.

We are entering a season of extraordinary enlightenment. We will experience the unveiling of Kingdom realities in an unprecedented way. Messages of truth and power will emerge with genuine authority to break strongholds and dominions within us, our churches, and our communities. We will taste *"the good word of God and the powers of the age to come"* (Heb. 6:5). Such messages will come from individuals who have personally encountered the Teacher. They will be people who have had their eyes and ears anointed for this purpose.

When these encounters begin to happen, God's people will put away false images just as they would impure cloth. They will discard lies and human precepts that were erroneously embraced as the Truth.

Such ones who will ascend the hill of the Lord and stand in His holy place are individuals with *clean hands and a pure heart, who have not lifted up their souls to falsehood nor sworn deceitfully* (see Ps. 24:3-4). They will not believe a lie, exchanging it for the truth, nor will they give a testimony of deception. The Holy Spirit's anointing will open their spiritual eyes and ears.

Recently during a prophetic conference, I asked the Lord why it is now important for us to have greater insight into heavenly light, sound, and color as observed by the disciple John in his revelations. During worship, the answer came in a clear and distinct manner: It facilitates and flourishes the depths of our agreement with Heaven and God's glory realm. The greater our comprehension of that realm, the more in agreement we will be with the things of the Spirit.

> *...That the God of our Lord Jesus Christ, the Father of glory, may give to you a spirit of wisdom and of revelation in the knowledge of Him. I pray that the eyes of your heart may be enlightened, so that you know what is the hope of His calling, what are the riches of the glory of His inheritance*

in the saints, and what is the surpass-
ing greatness of His power toward us
who believe. These are in accordance with
the working of the strength of His might
which He brought about in Christ, when
He raised Him from the dead, and seated
Him at His right hand in the heavenly
places (Ephesians 1:17-20).

When the eyes of our heart are flooded with light, we will begin to comprehend and understand the hope to which He has called us. We will perceive with greater clarity the glorious inheritance and the immeasurable and surpassing greatness of His power toward all who believe.

We will be able to do this as we become more conscious of the heavenly places in which God's saints reside and as we experientially apprehend the reality of being seated with Christ. Our spiritual senses will become more acclimated to that domain and perceptive of our heart's desire for the Father of lights.

ENDNOTES

1. Strong's Exhaustive Concordance, *yeshuash,* 3444.

2. Vine's Dictionary, a reference to Strong's, *chazah*, 2372.

Chapter 5

LIVING IN A
PROPHETIC
GENERATION

Something of significant spiritual consequence is on the horizon that will require our discernment and insight be taken to a new and deeper level. Greater sensitivity will be necessary in order to faithfully appropriate stewardship of the new things God will bring.

We have been—and will continue to be—in a learning process as we develop and flow more completely with the Holy Spirit. As always, the Lord gives us grace for our mistakes, but He is also calling us to mature and come up higher. Prophetic standards among believers must advance to a God-pleasing level so that we may become light in this dark world and provide clear direction to a lost generation.

On one notable occasion, the prophet Samuel stood before the people of Israel as a credible voice and representative of God. His words did not fall to the ground nor did he beg for his bread and sustenance. When he shared his revelations, people listened attentively to the validity of His voice, because he had cultivated a genuine exchange with God. That is the position we must maintain in this crucial hour. It is time for the prophetic ministry in the Body of Christ to emerge with a credible and trustworthy voice to address the notable issues presently unfolding in this generation.

OUR PROPHETIC PROMISE

The Scriptures underscore the end-time generation as one flowing in the prophetic power of the Holy Spirit (see Joel 2:28). This is one of the most exciting aspects of God to be uncovered in our day. The very nature of revelatory ministry involves communication and fellowship with the Lord in its fundamental functioning. It is the sharing of the mind of Christ and the discovery of the Lord's many and varied glorious attributes through the anointing of the Holy Spirit, who opens eyes to see and ears to hear. Just as it is written:

> *"Things which eye has not seen and ear has not heard, and which have not entered the heart of man, all that God has prepared for those who love Him." For to us God revealed them through the Spirit; for the Spirit searches all things, even the depths of God* (1 Corinthians 2:9-10).

Over the last few years, there have been various publications and articles addressing the prophetic nature of the present time. Some use terminology like "prophetic fad" or "a prophetic wave" to describe what is emerging. Our present call to revelatory ministry is neither a fad nor a wave. Rather, it is an integral part of our spiritual DNA, which is woven into the very essence of our Christian faith. We have the incredible privilege to be given access to the mind of Christ, and that potential is approached through the Spirit of Revelation. Having access to Jesus' mind, we are able to prophesy His thoughts and desires concerning individuals, congregations, regions, and nations.

Recently, I have been using the term *prophetic ministry* less and *revelatory ministry* more. In Scripture, we are promised entrance to the mind of Christ through the Spirit of Revelation. The very essence of prophetic ministry involves perceiving the articulation and understanding of God's mind. It allows the rite of passage into the depths of God. Our invitation promises a rich journey with God that brings Heaven to earth through people who become living tokens of His excellent design for humankind.

This unmerited gift grants access to God's thoughts and ways, which will always remain consistent with His Word. When our messages have come fresh from the heart of God, they will be saturated with the Spirit and Life. Endued with divine virtue, our words will not return void without having accomplished their fruitful purposes.

Accessing Heaven through greater awakenings to the realm of the Spirit offers a bountiful source of enlightenment and encouragement. God is not only yearning to be believed; He is breathlessly waiting to be experienced through life-changing encounters that can range from joyful and engaging to awe-inspiring and overwhelming.

REVELATORY BENEFITS

Many benefits come with the revelatory gifts of God:

1. We begin to understand our inheritance in Christ—the hope of our calling and the unfathomable riches of His glory—by the Spirit of Wisdom and Revelation (see Eph. 1:17-18).

2. Prophetic revelation provides strategic insight and guidance to the saints of God.

3. Paul's epistles teach us that the proper execution of revelatory ministry can generate conviction, repentance, and restoration.

4. The Holy Spirit's prophetic inspiration will guide us into all truth and

unveil the mysteries of the Kingdom reserved for this age.

5. According to the promise recorded through the prophet Isaiah, our spiritual offspring will be taught about God, and their well-being will be great. In addition, we will be established, kept from oppression and terror (see Isa. 54:13-14).

6. The prophetic anointing will also provide supernatural insight into the issues of life; it will break the bonds of confusion and oppression that keep humans bound to their fallen nature.

All this and much more are the heritage given through the revelatory attributes of the Holy Spirit. The needs and demands of this present time require wisdom from above. Even the noblest expressions of human ability pale in comparison to the wisdom of God! God's counsel is essential for our spiritual and natural well-being and prosperity.

LIVING IN A PROPHETIC AGE

At the beginning of each year, the Holy Spirit grants a commission to many in the prophetic community that will characterize much of what we do as a ministry throughout that year. At the outset of 2001, the Holy Spirit admonished us to begin sharing the biblical message of why we are living in a prophetic age.

The Lord began to show me how a large segment of the Body of Christ does not yet embrace the prophetic nature of our present time. Still, others have placed their faith in the prophetic Gospel primarily because of the successes of various ministries who were prophetic in nature. Their confidence was established more in the minister than in the Truth of God's Word. However, people may fail, but God's Word can never fail. Therefore, the Lord desires for people to see from the Scriptures their revelatory heritage and the fullness of this great privilege given to God's covenant people.

The Bible promises that to each is given a measure of faith (see Rom. 12:3). The question remains: *To what will we attach our faith?* Many have placed their faith in the economy, the government, medicine, organizations and institutions, and various other programs. However, the only secure place in which our faith can be fashioned is in the Lord and His Word. When the battles of life are raging, our only place of security is in Him and in His promises to us through His Word. This Truth will be especially applicable in the coming days as we approach the harvest of all seeds. The seeds of darkness will come to maturity; the Church must be in a position to overcome darkness rather than to be overcome by it.

Light and life are our spiritual heritage imparted by God's Word and by prayer. A generation of warriors is emerging who knows what they believe and why they believe it. Since the Bible prophetically points to this day, then the Bible will also provide our strategy for living and prospering both spiritually and naturally in the turbulent times foreseen by the prophets.

AN EARLY CHURCH MODEL

Tertullian was an apostolic father who stands out as a remarkable leader and scribe of early Church activity. He was recognized as a powerful thinker and writer at the dawn of the third century. He lived predominantly in the area known as Carthage (near Tunis, Tunisia, today) and fully embraced the impartation of prophetic gifts demonstrated in his generation, some 200 years after Pentecost.

In one of his writings, Tertullian describes a particular sister in his fellowship who was significantly gifted and privileged to witness many visions and visitations:

> We have now among us a sister whose lot it has been to be favored with sundry gifts of revelation, which she experiences in the Spirit by ecstatic vision. She converses with angels, and sometimes even with the Lord; she both sees and hears mysterious signs; some hearts she understands and to those in need she distributes remedies.

> Whether in the reading of the Scriptures, or in the chanting of Psalms, or in the preaching of sermons, or in the offering up of prayers, in all these religious services, matter and opportunity are afforded her of seeing visions. After the people are dismissed at the conclusion of the sacred services, she is in the regular habit of reporting to us whatever she may have seen in vision (for all her communications are examined with the most scrupulous care, in order that their truth may be probed).

Among other things, says she, "There
has been shown to me a soul in bodily
shape and a spirit has been in the habit
of appearing to me; not, however, a void
and empty illusion, but such as would
offer itself to be grasped by the hand, soft
and transparent and of an ethereal color,
and in form resembling that of a human
being in every respect."[1]

Tertullian continued to acknowledge this was her
testimony, and, as he put it, "for her witness there was
God, and as the apostle most assuredly foretold, there
were to be spiritual gifts in the Church."[2] This early
example of the Holy Spirit's visitation to His Church
releasing insight with understanding provides a pure
model for our hope and expectation for this hour as
well.

YOU MAY ALL PROPHESY

According to the apostle Paul, all believers inherently have in them the ability to prophesy (see 1 Cor.
14.1). He hoped that all of us would prophesy. The same
is not said of many other spiritual gifts. Nonetheless,
something is inherent in each believer as a common
denominator that allows each to prophesy.

As believers, it is our right, prerogative, and admonition to be endowed with the Spirit of Revelation. The Spirit of Revelation grants us insight into the mind of Christ, thereby allowing each person to prophesy. Thus, giving a prophetic word to someone is simply sharing the mind of Christ for that individual. Hearing God's voice is a fundamental covenant blessing available to every believer. Our adversary has fought diligently to keep this truth from becoming a living reality.

Being able to prophesy is a wonderful blessing, but it is only one of the many benefits that the Spirit of Revelation brings to believers. Over the last decade, personal prophetic ministry has been used to awaken the Church to a greater awareness of the importance of prophetic ministry. Still, the most important function of the Spirit of Revelation is to allow perpetual dialogue and fellowship with the Holy Spirit and an ability to access God's thoughts, secrets, and mysteries.

The Lord is willing to share secrets with His friends—those who have become trustworthy stewards. Through the Spirit of Revelation, the Lord freely gives us the ability to mine the depths of God's thoughts and desires for His people.

At the present time, our primary mandate is to begin to manifest the Kingdom of Heaven on earth. Our definition of this commission is simply: the Lord Jesus Christ, living and abiding in His people and doing through them the works that He did while on the earth in human form. In essence, this is the Kingdom! As His Body, we are the instruments by which the Lord has chosen to express Himself on earth. All creation is groaning for us to become all that God has ordained us to be. The redemption purchased at the cross of Calvary has provided the way for this incredible mandate to become a living reality.

In Joel 2, the prophet foresees and foretells the attributes associated with the future bride and the endowments of Heaven imparted to God's people. The infancy of the impartation took place on the day of Pentecost, yet the commission remains pertinent in these last days. As quoted through Peter:

> *But this is what was spoken of through the prophet Joel: "And it shall be in the last days," God says, "That I will pour forth of My Spirit on all mankind; and your sons and your daughters shall prophesy, and your young men shall see visions, and your old men shall dream dreams" (Acts 2:16-17).*

Visions, dreams, visitations, and heavenly experiences are part of our rich heritage and must flow in these last days. The more deeply we are entrenched in the Word, the higher we can soar in the Spirit to experience God. The prophet David once wrote that his heart would fail if he did not believe he would see the goodness and glory of God while in the land of the living (see Ps. 27:13). While on this side of eternity, David yearned for and expected to encounter God and engage the glory realm of Heaven. That longing for God's supernatural reality should likewise be the echo of our hungry generation.

HEARING HIS VOICE

In Revelation 3:20, through the admonition given to the Laodicean Church Age, the Lord states that He is standing at the door knocking. Whoever hears His voice and opens the door to Him, will dine and have fellowship with Him. The essence of His promise can be more fully understood by reading the great blessing given to the Zadok priesthood for their faithfulness during times of apostasy (see Ezek. 44).

The sons of Zadok were awarded the awesome privilege of ministering to the Lord and dining at His table—which speaks of intimacy and personal exchange from which they were able to discern God's heart for their generation. We will obtain this same perspective as we respond to His voice and open the door of fellowship.

Certainly, the key is more fully apprehended by understanding how God gives expression to His *voice*. In Daniel 9 we discover a secret that helps give definition to the identification of His voice:

> *To the Lord our God belong compassion and forgiveness, for we have rebelled against Him; nor have we obeyed the voice of the Lord our God, to walk in His teachings which He set before us through His servants the prophets* (Daniel 9:9-10).

Careful scrutiny of this prayer illustrates that the Lord's voice came through the prophets. These Old Testament prophets were blessed with special endowments of power from the Lord to stand as Heaven's representatives. They were anointed with the Spirit of Wisdom and Revelation that enabled them to be the Lord's spokesmen. Because of the anointing of divine insight and spiritual understanding, they were God's voice to people.

Today every believer, according to Ephesians 1:17-18, is now privileged to hear the Spirit of Wisdom and Revelation. The Spirit of Revelation represents God's voice by bringing illumination to God's Word and by communicating through various means found in Scripture. God is standing at the door and knocking by releasing a clear word to the Body of Christ through the Spirit of Revelation. Those with eyes to see and ears to hear His voice will open the door to Him and embrace every word that proceeds from His mouth. What is coming forth is a prophetic message concerning God's thoughts for this generation.

With the Old Testament prophets, anointing rested for a season and then lifted. However, when Jesus came to earth and was baptized by John the Baptist, the Scriptures declare the Spirit of the Lord descended and remained. The Holy Spirit's abiding enables God's covenant people to access the resources of Heaven and hear His voice.

When the Spirit of the Lord would visit the prophets of old, they would function in the Spirits of Wisdom and Revelation, Counsel and Might, Knowledge and Fear of the Lord. However, Jesus introduced a new day by His atoning death and resurrection, and the seven Spirits of God rested in and remained upon Him. He is now releasing that blessing back to His Church to be anointed once again with the sevenfold Spirits of God. (See Isaiah 11:2.)

Open the Door of Your Heart

The Lord is using the Spirit of Revelation to knock on the door of His people's hearts so they may know Him intimately. He desires a deep relationship with each of us, transcending even our highest expectations. As we embrace His voice and open our spirit to the revelatory realm, we will enter into divine communion and become transformed into His image.

> "I was asleep but my heart was awake. A voice! My beloved was knocking: 'Open to me, my sister, my darling, my dove, my perfect one! For my head is drenched with dew, my locks with the damp of the night'" (Song of Solomon 5:2).

In the Song of Songs, God offers us a prophetic and poetic picture of the bride and the bridegroom. While the bride is spiritually sleeping, her spirit is awake and hears the *voice* of the bridegroom. This portrait conveys the Lord's deep love for His bride and the prophetic whisper of His voice to awaken her from slumber, allowing her to enjoy the pleasures of being with Him.

ENDNOTES

1.   Terullian, *Latin Christianity: Its Founder Tertullian* (Peabody, MA: Hendrickson Publishers, 1994).

2.   Ibid.

Chapter 6

ATTRIBUTES OF THIRD HEAVEN REVELATION

O ur generation stands on the threshold of experiencing a spiritual restoration that will equate in prominence with the recovery of the Jewish people to the land of Israel. Scriptures that refer to the various signs of the times explicitly point to this reality. The prophet Isaiah foresaw this natural and spiritual restoration and announced:

Thus says the Lord, "In a favorable time I have answered You, and in a day of salvation I have helped You; and I will keep You and give You for a covenant of the people, to restore the land, to make them inherit the desolate heritages; saying to those who are bound, 'Go forth,' to those who are in darkness, 'Show yourselves.' Along the roads they will feed, and their pasture will be on all bare heights. They will not hunger or thirst, nor will the scorching heat or sun strike them down; for He who has compassion on them will lead them and will guide them to springs of water" (Isaiah 49:8-10).

This apostolic reformation will ignite the reestablishment and functioning of the Church in genuine spiritual power and authority. From this foundation, the Church will be able to soar to even greater places in God that await us—the Melchizedek priesthood and a deeper apprehension of being sons and daughters who have overcome and discovered rest in God. As the writer of Hebrews emphasized:

For if Joshua had given them rest, He would not have spoken of another day after that. So there remains a Sabbath rest for the people of God (Hebrews 4:8-9).

The apostle Paul was entrusted with notable understanding regarding the Holy Spirit's strategy in leading the Church. Paul's epistles clearly outlined the many offices established in God's government, as well as the various gifts and prophetic impartations of visions and revelations. Likewise, Paul demonstrated powerful teachings that came by the revelation of Jesus Christ and were affirmed with divine power (see Gal. 1:12). All of this, and more, will be fully operating in the days ahead.

Many saints will be given opportunity to experience God in ways articulated by the apostles Paul and John and the notable forerunners of old. Biblical prophecies pointing to the end-time generation highlight a people anointed with the Holy Spirit that will witness numerous events and Kingdom affairs through visions, dreams, and spiritual encounters. Many will also be taken into the third Heaven, and like Paul, experience God's realms that are impossible to communicate. With this invitation, the Lord is revealing Himself in fresh and profound ways by opening our eyes and ears to the eternal realm of God.

Revelation of His Attributes

One of the most captivating principles in walking with God is the revelation of His many glorious attributes. It has always been fascinating to discover throughout Scripture the diverse reactions of the Lord's servants when He manifested Himself through "eyes and ears" opened to that heavenly arena. For instance, following Jesus' death, burial, and resurrection, He appeared to His bewildered disciples as a loving Friend. Luke 24 highlights this wonderful encounter: The disciples were gathered, as two excited disciples shared their supernatural visitation on the road to Emmaus (see Luke 24:13-35).

While these things were being shared, Jesus Himself stepped into their midst with a salutation of peace and friendship. Very quickly, their startled reaction turned to joy as He encouraged them by saying:

> *Why are you troubled, and why do doubts arise in your hearts? See My hands and My feet, that it is I Myself; touch Me and see, for a spirit does not have flesh and bones as you see that I have* (Luke 24:38-39).

One can only speculate at the sheer elation that must have surged through each disciple, as each was warmly invited to embrace the resurrected Christ. This loving revelation of His attribute as the Friend and Master galvanized His disciples' hearts with an eternal bond of affection and loyalty. Jesus demonstrated His ability to appear in such a way His followers were not overwhelmed by the sheer power of His presence. Our Lord's revelation as Friend disclosed one attribute of His great character and forever altered the lives of His disciples.

FALLING LIKE A DEAD MAN

On the other hand, the beloved disciple John—the very one who once had laid his head upon the breast of God—also encountered this same Christ, but with revelation of different aspects of His attributes. In Revelation 1, we discover the Lord Jesus manifesting Himself to John as the Great Judge. So overwhelming was this experience that when John saw the Lord he *"fell at His feet like a dead man"* (Rev. 1:17). That was the apostle's reaction when beholding the revelation of Jesus as the Just Judge. Although Jesus was the same Person, the different manifestation of His attribute produced an entirely different response from the apostle!

A similar pattern can be found throughout Scripture. Moses established a face-to-face relationship with the Lord and spoke with Him as a friend. I cannot think of a more extravagant honor conferred to anyone. Even so, the Lord introduced Himself before Israel with such virtue and overwhelming demonstrations of His creative power that it produced great fear, even in Moses' heart (see Heb. 12.18-21).

So while the reactions vary, deeper revelations of God's attributes always are powerful and awe-inspiring. In our generation, we are being offered an open door to the Spirit's realm that is truly exceptional in its excellence. Moreover, it is one that must be administered with solemn care and reverence.

As never before, we must learn to discern the Lord's true voice. Likewise, a clear distinction must be developed to rightly differentiate the proper authority level and dimension of our spiritual experiences. Clearly, the Lord desires to touch and embrace us. Nevertheless, we should be careful not to call things "throne room" revelations and visitations that are not from that lofty place.

Our directive is to guard, through the Holy Spirit, the great treasure entrusted to us. We cannot afford to devalue our spiritual currency at this crucial stage, nor abort or even delay the marvelous opportunity to experience divine treasures.

UNPRECEDENTED OPPORTUNITIES

We are living in a day unprecedented in history. Great and divine opportunities are imminent as many mysteries of the Kingdom are beginning to unfold. The prophet Daniel foresaw this day and was instructed to seal the revelation of his vision for *"the time of the end"* (Daniel 12:4 NKJV). We are living in that day, and the seal is being lifted on the revelation of end-time promises.

One of the most notable opportunities being given to God's Church today is the "open door" presented in the Book of Revelation:

> *After these things I looked, and behold, a door standing open in heaven and the first voice which I had heard, like the sound of a trumpet speaking with me, said, "Come up here, and I will show you what must take place after these things"* (Revelation 4:1).

A body of righteous believers is being given the invitation to "come up here" so God can disclose things that will be taking place in this generation. There are many followers of God who are earnestly calling upon the Lord, corporately and individually.

> *Call to Me, and I will answer you, and show you great and mighty things, which you do not know* (Jeremiah 33:3 NKJV).

A careful examination of the language contained in this passage indicates that what God will show us is hidden truth—wisely set apart for a specific time in God's scheme of things. As we call to Him, He promises to "show" us awesome things through eyes that see and ears that hear in the Spirit. This is a divine invitation that cannot be approached carelessly, presumptuously, or flippantly. It is a sacred and holy mandate that must be addressed with the greatest reverence and awe.

As a part of our lofty assignment, we shall be equipped with the discernment and maturity to recognize a forged imitation presented with the intent to deceive. The manna reserved for this day to unfold the Kingdom of Heaven is of priceless value. The one whose misguided desire is to *"be like the Most High"* (see Isa. 14:14), will attempt, with keen earnestness, to keep us from the Truth by appealing to the imagination and wounds of people in the arena of the soul.

It is our devoted pursuit to encounter God in ever-deeper dimensions by responding to the incredible liberty being introduced. On a personal level, that has been my daily prayer for over 14 years. This revelation transformed my life in 1989, when I discovered that door of opportunity. It was overwhelming to me, and remains so today, to think that the Creator of the universe would give me, or any person, an invitation and opportunity to encounter God in a face-to-face exchange. Even so, we want the truth and fruit of genuine third-Heaven encounters, which are grounded in the Scriptures, bearing the seal and endorsement of God.

OUR WARNING

No doubt, history will support that our adversary will attempt to propel this reality beyond its prescribed biblical parameters. That has been his modus operandi over the millennia. Faithful stewardship of God's purposes is a great responsibility that falls upon those who are pursuing the deepest dimensions in God.

Both the Scriptures and Church history provide illuminating attributes and fruit generated from encountering the Lord in such an awesome way. Both can serve as a gauge of the authenticity of a third-Heaven experience and to separate out the excessive and fanatical.

One of the most-often quoted passages in Scripture involves the righteous prophet Isaiah and his opportunity to ascend to the third Heaven and encounter God in a "throne room" experience. He records:

> *In the year of King Uzziah's death, I saw the Lord sitting on a throne, lofty and exalted, with the train of His robe filling the temple* (Isaiah 6:1).

His response to such an experience is quite revealing:

> *Then I said, "Woe is me, for I am ruined! Because I am a man of unclean lips, and I live among a people of unclean lips; for my eyes have seen the King, the Lord of hosts"* (Isaiah 6:5).

Because of his humility, an atoning provision was offered that provided the cleansing he needed to stand in this place.

Much is written about this notable prophet and his standard of righteousness and commitment to God. Both the Scriptures and history record Isaiah's stand against the apostasy and infidelity of God's covenant people. In fact, it is commonly believed that his position of purity to the truth cost him his life. It is generally accepted and recorded in the Apocrypha that his body was "sawn asunder," because he refused to compromise.[1]

By no means do I suggest that access is granted to this heavenly domain by virtue of any works or personal merits. Rather, it is by the grace of God and our willingness to yield to the consecrating work of the Holy Spirit.

Likewise, such an opportunity is not approached carelessly. It requires devoted stewardship. There are many who are pursuing this worthy goal in corporate meetings. Nonetheless, my counsel is to be observant that the genuine does not get lost in the counterfeit. The judicious administration of divine aspects in Him will require governmental oversight from those anointed with the Spirit of Wisdom and Revelation.

The evidence and fruit of Isaiah's experience is vividly portrayed in this biblical account. Clearly, Isaiah had been given the privilege of seeing numerous visions and revelations of the Lord in his office as prophet. He was functioning in his prophetic calling long before his visit to the throne of Heaven. Even so, the power and unveiling of God in this experience left Isaiah, according to his own words, "undone" and "ruined" (see Isa. 6:5). It no doubt left an indelible mark on his life and character.

ENDNOTE

1.   The Martyrdom of Isaiah, The Apocrypha and Pseudepigrapha of the Old Testament, R.H. Charles Oxford: Clarendon Press, 1913. Wesley Center Online; http://wesley.nnu.edu/biblical_studies/noncanon/ot /pseudo/amartis.htm.

Chapter 7

EQUIPPING WARRIORS

O ur national military has now developed sophisticated high-tech weaponry that is off-the-charts in its versatility and effectiveness. That is a natural indication of a spiritual reality. What an incredible waste it would be, of both personnel power and armament, if our armed forces took rookies, fresh out of boot camp and outfitted them with these weapons and sent them to the frontlines. Most likely, they would be killed and the valuable weapons lost.

So it is in the Lord's Kingdom. Growth and maturity are required to be entrusted with "advanced weaponry" so warriors are not needlessly killed or the weapons lost. With mass media and all the varied and simple means at our disposal to approach the frontlines, it would be virtually effortless for people with developing gifts to engage the enemy in a realm beyond their maturity and scope of authority.

The Lord loves us and has plans for our welfare and not our calamity or demise. He has provided imperative equipping ministries to teach us how to develop in our gifts and callings, and to discover the Lord's weapons and how to use them prolifically and how to temper our zeal with wisdom. The Lord's governmental design will provide:

> ...*For the equipping of the saints for the work of service, to the building up of the body of Christ* (Ephesians 4:12).

The term "equipping" in this passage is *katartisismos*, denoting "to make fit" and implying a process leading to consummation...a fitting or preparing fully and perfecting; to be fully furnished.[1] This expression emphasizes a work to be taken to its completion without leaving that place until fully furnished.

In our development, we also discover His intimacy and fellowship as we cultivate exchange with Him and learn to hear His voice, then we will not follow another shepherd. This is a wonderful arena that should not be hurriedly departed. It would be like Paul and Barnabas, who while praying and ministering to the Lord, were set apart by the Holy Spirit and sent. Then, it is the Lord's bidding, and He will cover and protect His purpose.

ROOTED AND GROUNDED

Indisputably our great desire is to soar in the Spirit and obtain revelations of God's nature, power, strategy, and insight. However, to best accommodate this great privilege, we must be firmly *rooted and grounded* in Him. As the Holy Spirit spoke to me while in a conference in Canada, "Go deep in order to go high."

We must be…

1. Rooted and grounded in love (see Eph. 3:17).

2. Rooted and grounded in faith (see Col. 1:23).

3. Rooted and grounded in truth (see 2 Tim. 3:15).

I cannot overemphasize the importance of these three foundations in order for us to be trusted with the Lord's secrets. We are living in a generation privileged to be endowed with the Spirit of Revelation leading us into comprehension of the mysteries of the Kingdom. To facilitate this in us, we must be established in truth, faith, and love to properly understand and appropriate His heart.

The more firmly we are grounded, the more capable we become to penetrate Heaven by the Spirit of Wisdom and Revelation and embrace insight with understanding. The pursuit of truth will lead us to places in the Spirit yielding the fruit of righteousness and power. The quest for knowledge without truth can result in pride and arrogance. A clear distinction between the two is essential for personal transformation and maturity. When we cultivate a love for truth, we will not be turned over to deluding influences... that will characterize those who have rejected Christ in the last days (see 2 Thess. 2:10-11).

IN THE SPIRIT

Currently, many believers are oppressed with feelings of hopelessness, fear, doubt, and other bondages that the enemy exploits. It is the purpose and desire of the Holy Spirit to carry believers above this realm, into the Spirit, where our blessings and provisions are discovered in Christ. In this higher realm, we embrace hope to displace hopelessness and fear is overcome by faith.

This truth is evidenced in both the Old and New Testaments. On one occasion, the prophet Elisha boldly encountered the armies of the king of Aram without timidity or reservation. Conversely, his servant was battling issues of fear and doubt. That is, until he was carried above that realm to discover the more accurate spiritual perspective. God's governmental leader helped his servant above the soulish realm of anxiety and uncertainty by saying...

> *Do not fear, for those who are with us are more than those who are with them. Then Elisha prayed and said, "O Lord, I pray, open his eyes that he may see." And the Lord opened the servant's eyes and he saw; and behold, the mountain was full of horses and chariots of fire all around Elisha* (2 Kings 6:16-17).

When the prophet prayed for his servant, the impartation of the anointing allowed the servant access to the realm of faith and supernatural vision. As a result, he was changed and his perspective radically transformed. The limited view this servant previously held is the only one his adversary, the devil, wanted him to comprehend. Likewise, the enemy desires that we see only the seemingly insurmountable obstacles and difficulties that stand between us and our destiny. Therefore, when we walk by the Spirit, we will not carry out the deeds of our fallen nature.

In Elisha's servant, this experience radically affected his life—his eyes were opened and he saw. In a similar way, the Holy Spirit desires that we carry this anointing that opens eyes and distinguishes between the deceptions of our adversary and the provision of our Redeemer. Experientially comprehending our Source unleashes supernatural faith to live above this worldly realm and access the heavenly dimension.

MARIA WOODWORTH-ETTER

Visions and revelations seemed to be an integral part of Maria Woodworth-Etter's ministry. This realm of the Holy Spirit was experienced by both those who were saved and others who attended the meetings to ridicule and mock her ministry. It is well documented that many saints who were bound by various forms of oppression and sickness were delivered through their supernatural encounter with the heavenly realm during these meetings.

In each meeting in which this dimension was opened, a reverential awe permeated the auditorium and forever changed each one touched. Many individuals who discovered that "open door" in her meetings made lifelong commitments to the Lord. It is reported that some actually received the gift of speaking other languages and were commissioned as missionaries to the nations.

Maria Woodworth-Etter reported that prophetic utterances concerning future events were given to young and old alike, many of which took place within days or weeks. Others returned with supernatural knowledge and insight they had no way of knowing within themselves.

In each case, people were captured by the humility and contrition demonstrated in the lives of those who encountered God in this deeper spiritual arena. No one boasted or acted superficially; only reverence, contrition, and a life of consecration to God was evidenced. Even so, great joy also characterized this remarkable woman's life and ministry.

In one particular meeting held in St. Louis, Missouri, the people of the city were particularly harsh in their treatment of this precious sister and her ministry team. The meetings were attended by some of the most hardened characters in the city. In her journal, Maria Woodworth-Etter wrote:

> Men stood on the seats with hats on, cigars and pipes in their mouths, coats off and sleeves rolled up...women wore dirty aprons...and bare armed...they would shoot off firecrackers and when we sang, they sang even louder and when we prayed, they clapped their hands and cheered. They carry pistols and clubs and were ready to kill us and tear down the tent.[2]

However, the end of her story is quite different. The Lord faithfully heard the prayers of His devoted saints and responded by opening the Heavens and giving people visions of Heaven and hell. Through the Holy Spirit, the people encountered a spiritual dimension. The results were stunning, according to Woodworth-Etter:

> The fear of God came upon the multitude. The sweat came on their faces and they

stood as though in a trance; men began to take their pipes out of their mouths and their hats off. The women began to cover their bare necks and arms with aprons. They felt they stood naked and guilty before God. They began to get off the seats (from standing) and sit down but some fell and lay like dead.[3]

Evidence of a tangible touch from the third Heaven was apparent and easily discerned. This was true both for those who were saved and those who were not. The fruit was visible through the people's responses and by its consistency with the Scriptures. Often, it is recorded in Maria Woodworth-Etter's writings that sinners and saints alike would cry out in reverential fear when the heavenly dimension was opened to them.

OUR HOPE

A phenomenal opportunity to encounter and embrace God is being given to the Church around the world today. It is one that must be welcomed and protected. It is my heart and ambition to encourage every believer to pursue this God-given reality. Nonetheless we must also emphasize the importance of discerning God's voice so that we are not deceived by another voice, nor identify something as being from the sacred realm that is merely an expression of our imagination.

ENDNOTES

1.   *Katartisismos*, Strong's 2677 and Vine's Dictionary referencing 2677.

2.   Maria Woodworth-Etter, *A Diary of Signs and Wonders* (Tulsa, OK: Harrison House Publications, 1980).

3.   Ibid.

Chapter 8

DISCERNING SPIRITUAL REVELATION

It remains imperative to recognize other sources of revelation that can—if not properly discerned—substantially hinder our ability to be effective. We are living in a day in which spiritual eyes and ears are being opened with unprecedented access and clarity. Even so, our adversary will often release deluding revelation from the heavenly places in which the forces of darkness dwell.

The enemy does this in an effort to circumvent and subvert the purposes of God designed to be executed in and through His Church. Naturally, there are non-Christians who contend against the Church and the work of the Holy Spirit. These would include, but are not limited to, practitioners of the occult, new age, and others.

The very fact that there is an awakening to spiritism provides evidence that we are living in the latter days. In his first epistle to Timothy, the apostle Paul warned about this reality, saying:

> But the Spirit explicitly says that in later times some will fall away from the faith, paying attention to deceitful spirits and doctrines of demons, by means of the hypocrisy of liars seared in their own conscience as with a branding iron (1 Timothy 4:1-2).

Therefore, it should be no surprise to us that interest and awareness have escalated in spiritual matters. Plenty of seducing spirits with deceptive motivations are being released in this day. This reality should not make us flee from the true realm of revelation, but embrace it all the more. When genuine revelation is present, it makes counterfeit revelation appear all the more corrupt.

As the Body of Christ, we are entreated to be cognizant that our adversary will attempt to cloud and disrupt the flow of insight we desperately need. That is not a feature to fear—only to identify and discern. We need not have a spirit of timidity toward revelatory ministry. Nonetheless, it would behoove us to embrace wisdom and knowledge when discerning the source of revelation.

> *Beloved, do not believe every spirit, but test the spirits to see whether they are from God; because many false prophets have gone out into the world* (1 John 4:1).

THE SOURCE OF REVELATION

Currently, the Lord is allowing many in the Church to see things taking place in the second Heaven as well as portions of His perfect plan in the third Heaven. The enemy would have people believe all is well, by calling good things as "evil" and base or foolish things as "good." Presently, a deceptive voice seeks to find an outlet to hinder the preparation of God's people for the end-time battle. This is explicitly detailed in Revelation 3:17-18:

> *Because you say, "I am rich, and have become wealthy, and have need of nothing," and you do not know that you are wretched and miserable and poor and blind and naked, I advise you to buy from Me gold refined by fire so that you may become rich, and white garments so that you may clothe yourself, and that the shame of your nakedness will not be revealed; and eye salve to anoint your eyes so that you may see."*

The second Heaven simply denotes the spiritual domain in which our adversary functions. In Ephesians 6:12, the apostle teaches us that we do not wrestle against flesh and blood but against spiritual adversaries in heavenly places. The phrase "heavenly places" is taken from the Greek word *epouranios*, which signifies a celestial or spiritual domain.[1]

We know that our adversary does not reside in a place as high as the Most High God because it was satan's desire to ascend to the heights of Heaven above God's throne. Paul spoke about a visitation he once had to the third Heaven. Therefore, the enemy of our soul temporarily maintains dominion over this world through a heavenly place lower than the third Heaven, which we call the second Heaven.

From the second Heaven, spirits of divination and sorcery attempt to masquerade as the Holy Spirit, creating disillusionment and discouragement in our camp. When people continue unknowingly to entertain revelation from the second Heaven, hopelessness begins to fill their hearts. In reality, it is the impartation of the plans of satan. It is imperative for the Church to understand this reality and be prepared for it.

In Isaiah 14:13-14 we discover the five "I will's" of satan. The fifth "I will" of satan was his misguided attempt to imitate God. In his declaration, satan said: *"I will make myself like the Most High"* (Isa. 14:14). This is the most dangerous of all. This aspect of our enemy's plan is to masquerade as the Holy Spirit and be as much like Him as possible, while imparting seeds of darkness and death. In Matthew 24:24 this spirit appears so convincing that it would deceive the very elect, if possible. Resident in the spirit of God's elect is an ability to discern this form of deception.

CONTEND FOR
THE BLESSING

Our enemy is not our fellow humans, but rather, the evil influences released in the earth that operate through men and women, vaunting against the purposes of God. The wise apostle Paul entreats us to bring correction gently to those in opposition, so perhaps God may grant repentance leading to the knowledge of the truth. Thereby, they may come to their senses and escape the snare of the devil (see 2 Tim. 2:25-26). That is our quest as well. The false spirit is so closely akin to the Holy Spirit, the Lord announced it would deceive the very elect if possible (see Matt. 24:24).

Spirits of delusion will introduce into the Church the spirit of the world and attempt to nullify the grace of God. The views of truth necessary to purify the Church are not those the world gives, but those that are communicated by the Spirit of God. Spirits of delusion will attempt to lead God's people away from the reality of the Kingdom expressed in the Book of Acts.

During the later years of his life, John G. Lake received a powerful angelic visitation. In this encounter, the angel opened the Scriptures to the Book of Acts saying,

> This is Pentecost as God gave it through the heart of Jesus. Strive for this...contend for this...teach the people to pray for this. For this, and this alone will meet the necessity of the human heart and this alone will have power to overcome the forces of darkness.[2]

As the angel departed, he admonished Brother Lake insisting:

> Pray, pray, pray...Teach the people to pray. Prayer and prayer alone, much prayer, persistent prayer, is the door of entrance to the heart of God.[3]

The Lord is prophetically indicating that He is going to release the Zadok or righteous priesthood to teach the distinction between the sacred and the profane (Ezek. 44:15-16). This ministry will be the government of God providing a cleansing light to purify the glorious bride of Christ. The prototype for this righteous priesthood is Melchizedek (which is Hebrew for "my King is righteous")—the Lord Jesus.

The primary purpose of deluding spirits is to veil the minds of those without faith so the light of the Gospel of the glory of Christ, who is the image of the invisible God, would not shine into them (see 2 Cor. 4:4). False prophetic spirits will announce the sufferings of Christ but not His glory. They will agree with Christ crucified but not Christ risen and the power of His resurrection. They will even promote the Gospel of God's grace but not the Gospel of Christ's glory. The preaching of Christ's glory elicits the greatest enmity from satan and is what he has worked so diligently to keep veiled from the eyes of the Church.

Simply having a zeal for God is not sufficient. Zeal must be accompanied with divine truth according to Romans 10:2-3. Sincerity alone is not adequate. With sincerity of heart, Uzzah reached his hand to steady the Ark of the Covenant, yet it cost him his life because it did not follow the Lord's protocol (see 2 Sam. 6:6-7). All of us can fall prey to the influence of seducing spirits when our works are performed as religious duties rather than out of a heart of passion for our Savior based in truth. By the grace of God, we are being compelled to return to the simplicity and purity of devotion to Christ.

Rightly Discerning the Word

A provision of Heaven is set aside for this generation that is unprecedented in its power and glory. However, to appropriate this gift properly, we must accept God's refining fire so we can recognize seeds of corruption in our soul that can hinder our ability to receive His heavenly resources. Spirits of deception will seek to convince people they are spiritually rich and complete, having need of nothing—when in reality they are in desperate need of God and His garments of salvation and righteousness.

We have an open invitation to come boldly before the throne of grace; yet the journey remains sacred and holy, requiring clean hands and a pure heart. The fruit of those who genuinely have their spiritual eyes and ears open and experience God in this way will be evident. Revelations and reflections birthed in the soulish imagination are likewise apparent. When people are moved by the inclinations of the soul, it opens the way for the imagination to formulate images and mental pictures that clearly do not carry the authenticity of third Heaven revelation.

Misleading messages can manifest through prophetic words of flattery and self-promotion. That is not to say that a word from the Lord is always correctional or chastening—quite the contrary. God is always pointing out areas needing grace and extraction, but with a spirit of reassurance and expectancy. His reproofs are galvanized in charity and comfort to our spirit—not necessarily to our flesh.

The anointing of the Holy Spirit helps us live above the realm of worldly influences that imprison us in doubt, discouragement, fear, rejection, and all the other attributes of the fallen nature. When we ascend and soar like eagles in the Spirit, we find our blessings of peace, hope, faith, and charity. Some leaders carry an anointing that can be imparted, to help individuals learn to walk in the Spirit.

Even so, this in itself does not constitute a third Heaven revelatory experience where the visions and manifestations of the Lord are obtained. Isaiah, Paul, and John record the virtue of the third Heaven, the awesome grandeur and awareness of God we desperately need. The Lord ardently desires for us to experience "deep calling unto deep." He is calling us to share in His nature.

In his letter to the Ephesians, the apostle Paul teaches:

Our struggle is not against flesh and blood, but against the rulers, against the powers, against the world forces of this darkness, against the spiritual forces of wickedness in the heavenly places (Ephesians 6:12).

The spiritual forces of wickedness in heavenly places have set themselves in opposition to the working of the Holy Spirit through God's people. Not only will this evil defiance create snares and traps for believers, but it will also assail our minds and spirits during seasons of prayer.

At times, it may seem we are easily able to move directly into the realm of the Spirit during prayer. At other times, it may seem as though all the forces of hell are opposing us as we attempt to come before the throne of grace in prayer and intercession. These difficult seasons are divinely allowed to train us in warfare and establish spiritual fortitude and a track record of victory as we wrestle with the enemy. God's intent in this is that we discover by small victories the power, authority, and amazing provision established for us in the cross.

To glean the nuggets God desires to show us often requires battling through intense spiritual resistance until we are able to soar above it and hear pearls He will express and see gems He is eager to disclose. To breakthrough victoriously requires diligence and determination through fervent prayer and intercession; not as striving but conditioning.

False prophetic ministry will also attempt to persuade people that it is useless to serve God in radical purity and faithfulness or to keep His Word earnestly. As stated in Malachi 3:15:

> *So now we call the arrogant blessed; not only are the doers of wickedness built up, but they also test God and escape.*

This deception will not be done with open words of rebellion but with subtle patterns of justification and blame-shifting that will inhibit the people's ability to stand righteously before God and share in His highest provision.

GREATER MEASURES OF REVELATION

A dangerous form of false prophetic ministry in the order of Edgar Cayce and Nostradamus is emerging in these last days. Even though some accurate information can be extracted from even false revelation, *true* revelation must be grounded in God's Word and acknowledged by the Holy Spirit's work through God's grace.

Paul dealt with this in his day when he recorded:

> *A slave-girl having a spirit of divination met us, who was bringing her masters much profit by fortune-telling. Following after Paul and us, she kept crying out, saying, "These men are bond-servants of the Most High God, who are proclaiming to you the way of salvation"* (Acts 16:16-17).

In this passage, we discover the apostle Paul rebuking the spirit of divination resident in the young slave girl, who had been prophesying accurately about Paul and Silas and their apostolic mandate. Apparently, the young girl's insight must have been genuine and impacting, as it brought much profit to her masters. Her deliverance actually initiated persecution against Paul and Silas from those who benefited from her false anointing.

In 1987, Bob Jones had a revelation concerning a second shuttle disaster in the U.S. space program that would indicate the timing of God and point to this very subject. Naturally, the Lord did not initiate the disaster. But when it occurred, it served as a signpost for the Church. I have attempted to locate documentation of this prophetic word but have been unsuccessful. I did, though, speak with another highly regarded international minister, Larry Alberts, who clearly recalls the prophetic word and confirmed the essence of it.

The heart of the message is that the second shuttle disaster will mark a time in which God will open the door of Heaven to grant access to the third Heaven and His throne room. The purpose of the message was to release substantial insight with understanding. Throne-room prophets will receive their revelation from that lofty third Heaven throne-room realm. This is an invitation. The second accident simply served as a signpost to indicate a spiritual reality.

A Prophetic Warning

A warning attended that word, however. With the accompanying increase of authority in godly revelations, there will be corresponding counterfeit anointings released as well. These forged anointings, in large part, will be in people with genuine gifts of revelation who allow their divine communication to be polluted and wrongfully administered. Balaam would be a further example of this form of prophetic presentation.

Careful examination of the Scriptures will disclose that Balaam possessed a genuine gift and was recognized as a prophet. Although possessing a clear prophetic gift, Balaam unfortunately used his gift and authority for selfish gain. This misuse of God's intent for the gifts happens when we employ true spiritual gifts through our soul rather than our spirit. Normally, this results from woundedness or when ambition, pride, and/or greed are present.

Balaam actually worshiped God with the proper method of sacrifice necessary for approaching God, as did Israel.

> *He said to them, "Spend the night here, and I will bring word back to you as the Lord may speak to me." And the leaders of Moab stayed with Balaam. Then God came to Balaam and said, "Who are these men with you?"* (Numbers 22:8-9)

When the princes of Moab attempted to employ Balaam, he persuaded them to lodge for the evening while he inquired of the Lord (Jehovah Adonai). The Bible declares that God (Elohiym) came to Balaam and spoke concerning Balak's request.

Unfortunately, as recorded in Second Peter 2:15, Balaam *"loved the wages of unrighteousness."* Balaam fell into the sin of covetousness, which God declares to be idolatry. The adversary had gained an advantage by appealing to his ambition and greed. The precious prophetic gift imparted to Balaam had become corrupted, and he is forever remembered as a stumbling block before God's covenant people. The Book of Revelation depicts this scenario as one that must be overcome to enjoy the blessings of the "victorious ones."

While the Scriptures clearly advise us to earnestly desire spiritual gifts, it is the spirit within a person using the gifts that is the distinguishing factor. The question must be asked, "Is it our heart to truly build the Kingdom of Heaven or to establish our name and individual ministry?" It is surprising how easily those two lines of demarcation can be blurred. History has proven that. We need the Holy Spirit to guard and protect our hearts from every form of corruption that would prostitute or merchandise God's priceless gifts.

FUNCTIONING AS SPIES

Obtaining prophetic warnings is an advantage of revelatory ministry. The Holy Spirit will provide enlightenment regarding the enemy's plans and strategies against the Church. As the apostle Paul openly declared, we do not wrestle against flesh and blood (see Eph. 6:12). Our contention is with principalities, powers, and spiritual wickedness in heavenly places. From that domain, plans and strategies are formulated against the work of God and His people.

Numerous prophetic people are presently being endowed with insight and understanding to discover and disclose the schemes of the adversary. This is an important weapon in God's arsenal for mobilizing troops for prayer and intercession to overcome satan's sabotages.

> Now the heart of the king of Aram was enraged over this thing; and he called his servants and said to them, "Will you tell me which of us is for the king of Israel?" One of his servants said, "No, my lord, O king; but Elisha, the prophet who is in Israel, tells the king of Israel the words that you speak in your bedroom" (2 Kings 6:11-12).

I have been intrigued by the many creative ways used by military forces to spy on their enemies. Often, the victory in a battle hinges on the validity and accuracy of intelligence information provided by spies. When an opposing force has insight into the plans and strategy of its enemies, the victories generally are assured.

This is also true in the spiritual battle taking place in our time. Our God is all-knowing and is willing to share His insight with us when we become trustworthy. He is willing to enlighten us to the plans of the enemy against specific individual lives, churches, cities, or conferences. By having this intelligence, our forces can be mobilized to counterattack through prayer and intercession and also identify the enemy's spies infiltrating our camp to disrupt and divide.

Elisha would torment the kings of Israel's enemies by relating to Israel's king the plans and strategies formulated in their private chambers. This spiritual principle is not only valid but immensely valuable in its application.

A NEW DAY DAWNING

The coming days will bring greater dimensions of darkness in the world; yet our hope is for the appearing of God's weighty presence. As emphasized in Revelation 3:20, the Lord stands at the door and knocks and to Him who hears and opens the door to his heart, the Lord will dine with him. This is an individual commission and requires an individual response.

It is imperative that we guard against doing so much *for* God, when our invitation is to do things *with* Him. Great value is placed in learning from our past mistakes. Many distinguished leaders have found themselves captured by doing things for God and unknowingly losing their sensitivity to the voice of His Spirit.

Our highest purpose is to have relationship with Him. Intimacy with the Lord is the essence of our design in Creation and the highest purpose in the restoration of all things. To walk with God in the "cool of the day" (see Gen. 3:8) is still our foremost aspiration.

The earth is entering into a season of travail. World systems will be powerless in responding to the needs that are about to be present in the earth. Even those obtaining revelation through spirits of divination are prognosticating essentially the same thing. Only when anointed with the Holy Spirit can the Church impart wisdom and revelation that will provide genuine light in this dark generation.

The day is fast approaching when the prophetic ministry of the Church, through the spirit of Elijah resting upon a company of people, will once again encounter the *prophets of Baal* in a Mount Carmel showdown. When the genuine is present, it makes the counterfeit appear all the more perverted. The Church should not fear to take the prophetic Gospel to the marketplace where our enemy is attempting—often successfully—to dominate. This generation is desperate for authentic spiritual representation from the Kingdom of Light.

In another Old Testament example, the 400 prophets of Ahab each received spiritual revelation containing measures of truth, yet the origin was a deceiving spirit the Lord allowed because of Ahab's and his leadership's unrighteousness. A true prophet of God, Micaiah, was then summoned who was able to soar above the deceiving spirit and receive a true revelation from God's heart (see 1 Kings 22:1-28). Spiritual discernment and a good foundation in truth clearly identify false revelation, thereby motivating the believer to press in all the more earnestly to receive the genuine.

The Spirit of Truth will render the false spirits of revelation powerless, as with Paul, Elijah, and other loyal servants of the Lord. Instead of their prophecies bringing numbness to us, those with the true revelatory mantle will precipitate immobility and disarray in the camp of the enemy. Light dispels darkness. Amen.

ENDNOTES

1.   *Epouranios,* Strong's 2032; http://strongsnumbers .com/greek/2032.htm.

2.   John G. Lake; taken from his sermon transcript. Recorded in *John G. Lake: His Sermons, His Boldness of Faith;* Kenneth Copeland Publications.

3.   Ibid.

Chapter 9

TO FILL THE EARTH
WITH HIS GLORY

One thing I have found fascinating about human history is the orchestration of God in the placement of key figures at strategic moments in time, to fulfill a specific destiny for which they were uniquely qualified. It is amazing how geniuses in military strategy seemed to be born at precisely the right moment to meet the challenges of their day.

137

Something was imparted to them that mystically drove them. Do individuals pursue their destiny, or does destiny pursue them?

The same scenario is also true in biblical history, as notable prophets, judges, and leaders emerged to lead Israel during diverse times of adversity, apostasy, prosperity, and war. Clearly, God's covenant people are born with seeds of destiny imparted to them to meet the challenges and strategy of Heaven for their day.

A GENERATION OF DESTINY

We're living in a time of revealing. In our generation, the Lord is creating and preparing a Body of emerging spiritual warriors who will meet the spiritual challenges and prophetic destiny ordained for our time and foretold in Scripture.

One of the greatest mandates of all time is to cooperate with the Holy Spirit and see the biblical directive in Numbers 14 fulfilled—to be the instruments by which God fills the whole earth with His glory:

> So the Lord said, "I have pardoned them according to your word; but indeed, as

*I live, all the earth will be filled with the
glory of the Lord"* (Numbers 14:20-21).

Until now, God's glory has been hidden to us. Yet
the whole earth is filled with God's glory—His goodness. It's the glory of God to conceal a matter, and the
glory of kings to search it out.

Like Abraham, the cry of our hearts is, *"My Lord,
if now I have found favor in Your sight, please do not pass
Your servant by"* (Gen. 18:3).

Our earnest desire and aspiration should be that
we become the chosen generation through which
the Lord will give revelation and expression of His
nature, character, and supernatural power so that
we may begin to fill the entire earth with His glory.
That alone would fulfill the awesome prayer outlined by Jesus when He prayed, *"Thy Kingdom come,
Thy will be done in earth, as it is in heaven"* (Matt. 6:10
KJV).

We have the incredible privilege of living in the
generation that will witness the unveiling of great mysteries and hidden secrets reserved for the end-time
generation (see Dan. 12:4). Thankfully, the Holy Spirit
is beginning to unleash "great and mighty things"
related to our prophetic destiny from the Scriptures

and imparting to us insight with understanding concerning the revelation of His glory.

THE REVELATION OF HIS THRONE

Three passages the Holy Spirit is highlighting in this hour are Esther 5, Revelation 4, and Isaiah 6. Each Scripture describes a king sitting on his throne, providing a prophetic picture for our day. Isaiah 6 has always offered a significant and moving account of the privilege given to Isaiah to witness the revelation of the Lord as King and the design of Heaven.

If there is a King and a throne, then there must be a Kingdom and dominion over which He rules. May this generation be heralds displaying the Lord Jesus Christ as the victorious King wielding ultimate authority and dominion. And may we be ambassadors for the revealing of our Messiah and the Kingdom of Heaven.

The prophet Isaiah was given the great opportunity of seeing Heaven's design before the throne of God as seraphim spoke one to another declaring, *Holy, Holy, Holy, is the Lord of Hosts...* (see Rev. 4:8). They were allowed to see demonstrations of His majesty and authority with their eyes and give expression to what they had seen. Their words began to fill the temple with smoke and glory as they witnessed with their eyes and expressed with their lips the revelation of God sitting upon His throne in absolute and perfect supremacy and sovereignty.

That is the fashion of Heaven God would have us transfer to earth: an atmosphere in which He can dwell, redolent of His nature and character. Isaiah saw with his eyes and heard with his ears the activity and atmosphere surrounding the throne of Heaven. Many will be given the same privilege today and be commissioned to return with a report of God's goodness and glory.

Isaiah saw the design of Heaven centered on the kingship and dominion of the Lord and the unveiling of His glory. He watched the privileged worshipers positioned about the throne who witnessed the nature and character of God's kingly authority. He was then directed to return to the covenant people of his time and convey the Kingdom revelation given to him. To fully appreciate Isaiah's experience, one required anointed eyes and ears to facilitate spiritual perception of heart and the healing long foretold.

The apostle John declares in his Gospel account that it was the Lord Jesus Christ whom Isaiah saw on that fateful day:

For this reason they could not believe, for Isaiah said again, he has blinded their eyes and he hardened their heart, so that they would not see with their eyes, and perceive with their heart, and be converted, and I heal them. These things Isaiah said because he saw His glory, and he spoke of Him (John 12:39-41).

Isaiah witnessed the unveiling of the Lord's throne, saw His glory, and prophetically spoke of Him. His experience highlights the importance of possessing divinely anointed eyes and ears in order to fully appreciate the Lord's redemption and the ultimate commission for His covenant people. It is the Lord's desire to heal His people and have them cooperate with Him in the unveiling of His Kingdom and the commission to fill the entire earth with His glory.

Even if we live during a season in which the Heavens are opened, it remains necessary to possess illumined eyes and quickened ears to comprehend the day of our visitation. The Son of God Himself walked the earth for 33 years. Three of those years attested to the most phenomenal miracle ministry in human history. Even so, only a small remnant realized the day of destiny in which they were privileged to live and the prophetic fulfillment they witnessed.

The apostle John recognized the spiritual stupor mentioned in the prophecies of Isaiah that rested upon the people. He rehearsed the rebuke first articulated by Isaiah to his generation, which also prophetically pointed to the one living at the time of Jesus' earthly ministry. In fact, that reproof applies to all generations who fail to perceive the day of their visitation.

John affirmed the need to possess anointed eyes and ears essential for the recognition of open-Heaven opportunities. The day of our visitation must be consolidated with an anointing upon our spiritual senses allowing us to identify and apprehend God's heavenly design. Without it, we would be like all the prior generations who aborted their opportunity to enter into the fullness of the Lord's plan and purpose. There was always a remnant who possessed humble and contrite hearts which qualified them to be sealed into the company of overcomers. Nonetheless, the corporate opportunity was lost.

MULTIPLIED GRAINS OF WHEAT

Throughout Jesus' earthly ministry, He made it clear that His commission was to convey the understanding and demonstration of the Kingdom of Heaven. He was sent to teach in the Jews' synagogues, proclaim the message of the Kingdom, and heal all manner of sickness and disease (see Matt. 4:23). We have the same commission today. Throughout the gospels we see Jesus continually teaching and manifesting His Kingdom and the attributes inherent in our heavenly Father. That is also our great commission.

The Lord Jesus gave the analogy of Himself as a grain of wheat. He taught that if a grain of wheat falls into the earth and perishes, it is for the purpose of bringing forth multiplied grains of wheat like the original seed.

> *Truly, truly, I say to you, unless a grain of wheat falls into the earth and dies, it remains alone; but if it dies, it bears much fruit* (John 12:24).

It is our high calling to emerge as one of the grains of wheat that begins to demonstrate and teach the Kingdom design in the earth. A present move of the Holy Spirit is to prepare a company of overcomers that will experience the revelation of His Kingship and convey that unveiling to the Body of Christ. This company's experience with God will facilitate the ushering in and birthing of the Kingdom of God in the earth.

For the sake of clarity, I have often defined the Kingdom as the Lord Jesus Christ living and abiding in His people, doing through His people the same and greater works as He did while on the earth in human form. This is the promised fulfillment of John 14:12. Jesus did only what He saw the Father doing and expressed only what He heard by supernatural utterance through anointed eyes and ears.

Chapter 10

OUR PROPHETIC
MANDATES

Part of the Great Commission is the harvest of souls in salvation and the demonstration of the Spirit's power in our generation. Another part is the ministry of deliverance to set the captives free and liberate prisoners from spiritual dungeons. Then there is the ministry of healing, including restoring the eyes of the blind, unstopping deaf ears, and making lame limbs whole; but it includes inner healing of wounds to the soul and the spirit, which can take many forms. These are all wonderful lofty purposes to which we devote ourselves in preparation and equipping.

But, in the process of pursuing the Holy Spirit's power and anointing, we also discover an even higher purpose for which we were created: to have intimate relationship and communion with Him. For most people, even some Christians, the Lord Jesus is not a living reality but an inference or an unapproachable influence in a far-distant domain.

He is often spoken or referred to in generalities or coined phrases—such as "the man upstairs"—and remains personally unknown to individuals. Creeds and dogmas are formulated from this form of thinking that convert our walk with the Lord from relationship to religion. We cannot love an ideal or express loyalty to an influence. Most people fail to consciously understand that the Lord is a Person who is present and ardently desirous of relationship and personal exchange.

Although there is a collective acknowledgment of the Lord's existence, there is nevertheless an overriding misperception that He is unknowable or unapproachable on a personal level. That deceiving influence in the Church must be overcome in this generation. It is a form of spiritual wickedness that keeps us from the knowledge of God. Comprehension of someone is best attained through intimate partnership and shared experiences. A holy dialogue—through spiritually granted access to hear His expressions and experience His Presence—promotes awareness of Him and energizes us from a dead religion to a living relationship.

We have the clear spiritual doctrine, verified through the Scriptures, that God can be known in personal. The pages of the Bible are filled with heroes of the faith who discovered this reality. We find God walking in the Garden with Adam, expressing Himself with Moses through a burning bush, talking with disciples on the road to Emmaus, meeting with His apostle on the way to Damascus and on the Isle of Patmos and promising to be with us, even in us until the end of the age. Personal encounters transform and equip us to function in the supernatural realms of Heaven and walk in God's anointing as well as to sustain that place of relationship and authority.

PERPETUATING THE ANOINTING

Far too often, many devoted saints throughout history who gave themselves to the work of ministry somehow lost the intimacy and communion that brought them consistent anointing and power. A loving Personality communicating with His people is a dominant theme throughout the Scriptures. Where He finds a place of receptivity among humans, He shares insight, direction, correction, encouragement, and promise through various manifestations of His Spirit.

Consequently, we must invest ourselves in intimate exchange and sacred fellowship with the Lord and be completely unwilling to compromise that relationship for any purpose. Notice the heart cry of the apostle Paul. Even after many years of powerful ministry, his passionate desire was to *"know Him and the power of His resurrection and the fellowship of His sufferings"* (Phil. 3:10).

Besides the Great Commission to bring the Gospel of salvation and power and the more important necessity of having intimate relationship and exchange with the Lord, a third mandate that is perhaps equally as important, is to be the agency through which the entire earth is to be filled with God's glory.

REVELATION OF HIS GLORY

The Lord descended upon Mount Sinai in all of His glory and power and desired to use Israel to begin to fill the earth with His glory. Unfortunately, they missed the mark. The Lord was so grieved with the unbelief and disobedience of the people that he was prepared to destroy the entire nation with the exception of Moses.

Because of Moses' intercession, the Lord stayed His hand of judgment but made a profound declaration:

> So the Lord said, "I have pardoned them according to your word; but indeed, as I live, all the earth will be filled with the glory of the Lord" (Numbers 14:20-21).

There must be a generation who cooperates with the Lord to fulfill this solemn oath given so many centuries ago.

It was the desire of the Lord to reveal Himself to the entire nation of Israel. The chief desire of His heart is still to present Himself to a holy nation and a royal priesthood and use them to fill the earth with His glory. Thus, our directive along with winning the lost and healing the sick is to participate with the Holy Spirit in filling the earth with God's glory.

THE YEAR KING UZZIAH DIED

To better understand this great mandate, we can glean key insights from Isaiah 6:

> *In the year of King Uzziah's death, I saw the Lord sitting on a throne, lofty and exalted, with the train of His robe filling the temple* (Isaiah 6:1).

The Lord wonderfully blessed King Uzziah until his heart was lifted up in pride. This presumptuous arrogance caused Uzziah to enter the Holy of Holies and attempt to offer incense upon the altar without the priestly anointing and consecration essential for this duty. For this grievous error, God struck Uzziah with leprosy, as observed on his forehead by the priests. (See Second Chronicles 26:16-23.)

According to Levitical law, when the priests identified leprosy on the forehead of a person, that person was pronounced unclean and required to cover his lips and cry "unclean, unclean." (See Leviticus 13:43-45.)

To comprehend the significance of King Uzziah's transgression, let us begin with the statement of the prophet Isaiah as he stood before the very throne of

God witnessing the exchange of the seraphim giving glory to God:

> *And one called out to another and said, "Holy, Holy, Holy, is the Lord of hosts, the whole earth is full of His glory. And the foundations of the thresholds trembled at the voice of him who called out, while the temple was filling with smoke." Then I said, "Woe is me, for I am ruined! Because I am a man of unclean lips, and I live among a people of unclean lips; for my eyes have seen the King, the Lord of hosts"* (Isaiah 6:3-5).

When Isaiah found himself not in the type and shadow on the earth but in the literal Holy of Holies in Heaven before God's throne, he clearly must have remembered the grotesque and distorted appearance of King Uzziah before his death. With that image in mind, Isaiah in essence stated, I am like Uzziah stricken with leprosy; I am likewise unclean and unworthy to stand in this Holy place.

A DIVINE PROVISION

Interestingly, an angel flew to the very place in which Uzziah was stricken, the altar of incense, and extracted a coal and applied it to the lips of Isaiah. There was an atoning provision for Isaiah. The Lord had made a redemptive provision allowing atonement and cleansing for the condition in which Isaiah found himself.

No correction of the statement was made by Isaiah that he was unclean. Rather, the Lord's atoning attribute altered the condition of Isaiah and made him cleansed and worthy to participate in the exchange of glory taking place before the throne of Heaven. Uzziah entered the Holy Place on earth with pride and presumption, while Isaiah appeared with lowliness and contrition.

FILLING THE TEMPLE WITH GLORY

Then I heard the voice of the Lord, saying, "Whom shall I send, and who will go for Us?" Then I said, "Here am I. Send me!" (Isaiah 6:8)

When Isaiah yielded himself to this commission, he heard the unusual instruction coming from the Lord concerning the eyes and ears of the people of his generation. They were to be rendered spiritually blind and deaf.

Grace was not given for that generation to see with their eyes nor hear with their ears God's unfolding plan of redemption and His determination to fellowship with a body of people on the earth, spreading Kingdom authority. Jesus emphatically quoted this passage in his discourse to the religious leaders during His earthly ministry as well. From among all the people living in Jesus' day, only a small remnant received the Messiah and the life He imparted (see Matt. 13:14-15; Mark 4:12; Luke 8:10).

As Isaiah's instruction continues, the Lord states *"lest they see with their eyes, and hear with their ears, and understand with their heart, and return and be healed"* (Isa. 6:10 NKJV). Healing occurs when our eyes and ears are opened and our hearts are permitted to understand. Healing is not merely the restoration of bodies and emotions, but more importantly, the restoration of the breach between God and humanity. That is why our adversary has so emphatically opposed the impartation of revelatory gifts.

We can only participate in this Kingdom plan when we "see" and "hear" with spirit eyes and ears, thereby eliciting comprehension to our hearts. This insight cannot be the mechanical articulation of words with merely an intellectual perception of the Almighty's sovereignty and glory. We are recruited when we are *overcoming* saints anointed with the Spirit of Wisdom and Revelation who view, comprehend, and experience the unveiling of God's kingly authority, dominion, and glory and give expression to it.

The prophet Isaiah was granted the great privilege of seeing Heaven's design at the throne of God as seraphim declared to one another: *"Holy, Holy, Holy is the Lord of Hosts"* (Isa. 6:3). They were allowed to see with their eyes demonstrations of His majesty and authority and give expression to it. Their words began to fill the temple with smoke and glory through the witness of their eyes and the expression of their lips the revelation of God sitting upon His throne in absolute and perfect supremacy and sovereignty.

As the seraphim gave glory to God and God received the glory due Him, more of His divine attributes emanated to them causing an even greater demonstration of praise and glory. This Kingdom exchange and heavenly design continued filling the atmosphere with the glory and illumination of God until the entire temple was saturated with the appearance and revelation of His glory.

That is the fashion of Heaven to be transferred to earth and our assignment—to create an atmosphere on the earth that is consistent with His nature and character in which He can dwell. If we can fulfill this mandate, all the other purposes and desires for which we long will naturally be established and achieved by His Presence and anointing resting in us.

Certainly, Isaiah must have been compelled to likewise participate in this exchange of glory, yet he recognized the unworthiness and impurity of his own lips to give glory to God in such a holy surrounding. Fortunately, the provision of Heaven purified him and removed his uncleanness, allowing him to give glory to God.

WHO WILL GO FOR US?

This commissioning of Isaiah was not as a prophet. The Scriptures plainly report that he was already functioning in the office of a prophet long before the experience of Isaiah 6. Perhaps Isaiah was being asked, *Who will go for Us?* to begin filling the earth with the glory of the Lord of hosts as witnessed in Heaven before God's throne.

Isaiah observed the atmosphere surrounding Heaven's throne. He saw Heaven's design created around the kingship and dominion of the Lord and the unveiling of His glory as seen by those witnessing the nature and character of His kingly authority. In a similar way, this same atmosphere must be created on earth in His people, for the Lord's dominion and Presence to be fully manifested in our generation. That is the will of Heaven being done on earth. It is the creation of the environment in which the Lord is able to dwell. This eternal atmosphere of glory and beauty provides a surrounding consistent with His divine nature and character.

THE REVELATION OF OUR HEARTS

Anointed eyes and ears grant access to the revelatory realms that provide insight with understanding into the Lord's goodness and His divine virtue. Repeated exposure to these realms makes them so natural and real to us that the experiences become a part of who we are and woven into the spiritual fabric of our existence. Prayers are then offered by the Holy Spirit through us that are consistent with the desire of God's heart as the Holy Spirit makes intercession through the redeemed. Not one of those prayers has ever been lost throughout the ages—all have been captured and held in Heaven.

Another angel came and stood at the altar,
holding a golden censer; and much incense

was given to him, so that he might add it to the prayers of all the saints on the golden altar which was before the throne.

And the smoke of the incense, with the prayers of the saints, went up before God out of the angel's hand. Then the angel took the censer; and he filled it with the fire of the altar and threw it to the earth; and there followed peals of thunder and sounds and flashes of lightning and an earthquake (Revelation 8:3-5).

In this passage, the Bible portrays the prayers and intercession of the saints as smoke or incense received and mingled with Heaven's incense. This passage illustrates that our words—spoken or tacit—have a tangible substance that can be seen and grasped in the spiritual realm, when coming from honest and sincere hearts anointed with the spirit of revelation and have an immediate acknowledgment in Heaven. It is our privilege to give God glory and God's desire to receive glory and honor for who He is.

And the four living creatures, each one of them having six wings, are full of eyes around and within; and day and night they do not cease to say, "Holy, holy, holy, is the Lord God, the Almighty, who was and who is and who is to come. And when the living creatures give glory and honor and thanks to Him who sits on the throne, to Him who lives forever and ever, the twenty-four elders will fall down before Him who sits on the throne, and will worship Him who lives forever and ever, and will cast their crowns before the throne, saying, Worthy are You, our Lord and our God, to receive glory and honor and power; for you created all things, and because of your will they existed, and were created" (Revelation 4:8-11).

THE PRAYER OF DAVID

According to the Scriptures, David was a man after God's own heart. He also recognized this high calling and even prayed that the entire earth would be filled with God's glory.

Blessed be the Lord God, the God of Israel, who alone works wonders. And blessed be His glorious name forever; and may the whole earth be filled with His glory. Amen, and Amen (Psalm 72:18-19).

With his prophetic eye, David was able to recognize the desire of God's heart to fill the earth with
His glory. Like David, our earnest prayer should be
not only to live in a generation that witnesses the
return of God's glory but also to participate in the
communication and release of His glory throughout
the earth. That is one of the highest purposes for our
redemption and one for which we are being prepared
and groomed.

Among the different aspects of each of the four
living creatures (see Rev. 4:7), the attributes of the eagle
seem to characterize this entire generation of overcomers. The Bible often uses eagles to symbolize God's
people. This analogy is especially applicable in
identifying the prophetic qualities of our heritage.
Eagles are able to soar higher than any other creatures and are gifted with phenomenal eyesight,
equipped with special filters on their eyes that
allow them to maneuver directly toward the sun
while evading encounters with predators. We must
do likewise and flee to the Son when engaged with
enemy confrontation.

The apostle Paul made it clear that we each have
the privilege and aspiration to be anointed with the
Spirit of Wisdom and Revelation (see Eph. 1:17-19). Part
of this great endowment is to allow the eyes of our

hearts to be illumined to see with comprehension the revelation of His Person and His kingship and give expression to it. Without clear illumination, we cannot fully participate in the articulation and release of our Creator's glory.

Yielding Our Will to the Father's Will

Presently, the Holy Spirit is seeking to enlist a company of people who will yield themselves fully to Him and submit their will to the Father's will. In so doing, we will open the door for the opportunity to be cleansed with the provision of Heaven, as was Isaiah, thus permitting our participation in letting the Holy One of Israel equip us to be used according to His will. This opportunity is not to be approached with pride or presumption nor in an unclean condition like Uzziah. It is for those who have fully embraced the Lamb's redemptive blood and the Father's refining fire and are willing to allow the Holy Spirit to consume everything within us contrary to the divine nature.

We will not be able to meet the challenges of our generation relying on someone else's faith. Concerning the message of truth he lived and taught, the apostle

Paul once stated, *"For I neither received it from man, nor was I taught it, but I received it through a revelation of Jesus Christ"* (Gal. 1:12).

For us to maintain faith, we must likewise experience the revelation of Jesus Christ for ourselves and become the instruments through which His glory is given voice and substance. Naturally, the Lord will use men and women in leadership positions to set us on the course of faith and truth. Nevertheless, our ultimate destiny rests in our own hands and our willingness to spend time with the Lord. This is done through His Word and in prayer and meditation. Waiting on the Lord cultivates intimacy and fellowship with Him, thereby allowing the Holy Spirit to open to us the ways of the Kingdom through the perception of our spiritual eyes and ears.

It is interesting to observe in the Scriptures that leprosy is generally not healed but cleansed. Leprosy was an external condition of defilement and uncleanness that reflected an inner-spiritual corruption and deterioration. A company of people will answer the invitation to be cleansed by the coals from the altar and will proceed to this high place of revelation and comprehension from which we can begin to give glory to God.

Chapter 11

TASTING THE GOOD WORD OF GOD

W e are living in the time of the "harvest generation." All the seeds deposited in the Garden of Eden are now coming to full maturity. Both the seeds of darkness and the seeds of light are developing and initiating an active response on our part. This will cause some who have straddled the spiritual fence between the wide path of worldliness and mediocrity or God's most excellent narrow lane to finally choose one path or the other in this heightened spiritual environment in which we presently live.

We must either be ignited or find ourselves overcome by darkness. The times will no longer allow for lukewarmness. The antichrist spirit is approaching full maturity in the earth. Likewise, the Spirit of Christ is maturing in the hearts of many who will demonstrate, through mighty expressions of spiritual authority and power, the overcoming victory He achieved.

The Lord has prophetically promised to establish a biblical government with apostolic authority necessary for the preparation of His end-time bride. This is a gift of God's grace we must embrace. We must come to covet the process of separating the precious from the worthless in ourselves first, which will allow us to taste *"the good word of God and the powers of the age to come"* (Heb. 6:5). The Lord can only trust us with the fullness of His rich power and Kingdom authority when our character and nature are consistent with His own.

To facilitate that spiritual objective, we must clearly recognize the Scriptures are not a matter of private interpretation but an expression of the Living Word. The Lord Jesus, on the eve of His crucifixion, prayed as High Priest that His disciples would be sanctified in Truth (see John 17:17). That prayer is of paramount importance in this hour as righteous leaders are being set apart to become vessels of glory who give expression to the mysteries of the Kingdom and the anointed Word for this generation! They will possess anointed eyes and ears that see and hear what the Lord is doing.

Such victorious leaders, in whom the refining process is complete, will be the "good shepherds" upon whom the favor of the Lord will be apparent. They will mark the restoration of the mature judges and counselors evident in the early Church. These leaders will possess the mind of Christ and will impart godly counsel essential for our spiritual well-being. The *shechinah* evidenced in their lives will bring the Word of God to life and make it a living presentation of heavenly reality.

The Church's leaders' previous lack of comprehension has greatly inhibited believers' ability to be the bright, shining light in this dark world. This is beginning to change. The Lord is bringing forth a people of great spiritual understanding who will become beacons of light in the midst of deep darkness.

Such leaders will surface from the process of separation and washing in Truth, anointed with Holy Spirit power and displaying the Lord's victory over demons, disease, and death. This span of time in which we seem to be suspended indefinitely is providing a season of preparation and purging for the ones being sanctified for this anointing and commissioning. We set our sights on the goal of this high calling as we lay aside all that would stand in the way of the incredible destiny for which we are privileged to participate.

WASHED BY THE WORD

It is currently the Holy Spirit's desire to establish in us the radical purity essential to enter the secret place of the Most High and union with Christ. The Holy Spirit is now focused on the cleansing and purifying necessary for believers to enter a higher dimension of anointing and relationship with God.

> *That He might sanctify her, having cleansed her by the washing of water with the word that He might present to Himself the church in all her glory, having no spot or wrinkle or any such thing; but that she should be holy and blameless* (Ephesians 5:26-27).

When the anointing of the Holy Spirit quickens the Word with life and power, truth is allowed to penetrate into the very fiber of our being, thereby transforming us into the likeness of Christ. When the ultimate process of sanctification has been achieved, we will be presented to the Bridegroom reflecting His glory. That is the high purpose of being washed by the water of the Word.

The Holy Spirit will identify issues within us contrary to His nature and quicken the Word of Truth to provide a divine alternative. When we embrace the revealed Truth with arms of faith, that truth will begin to change our nature and character by creating purity and a Christ-like mind.

The mark of genuine goodness manifests a consecrated life. This takes place when our thoughts and ways have become consistent with His, as expressed in His Word. It is in the possession of the mind of Christ that we discover the secrets of His Kingdom and embrace the keys that unlock the vast resources of our promised inheritance.

> *Be anxious for nothing, but in everything by prayer and supplication with thanksgiving let your requests be made known to God. And the peace of God, which surpasses all comprehension, shall guard your hearts and your minds in Christ Jesus* (Philippians 4:6-7).

A place of peace and rest is available in God that serves as a guard or garrison over our hearts and minds. The term "guard" is taken from the Greek *phroureo* meaning to protect by a military guard or to prevent a hostile invasion or a siege.[1] A spiritual watch is divinely assigned to govern and express the pure and powerful qualities of God inherent in the Living Word.

THE ZADOK PRIESTHOOD

An emerging group of leaders prophetically exemplifies the Zadok priesthood portrayed in Ezekiel 44. This distinguished division of the priesthood remained faithful to the Word of God during times of apostasy and infidelity. For their faithfulness they were rewarded with a divine invitation to minister to the Lord at His table. As they emerged from that divine intimacy and fellowship, they were commissioned to teach God's people the difference between the sacred and the profane and to extract the clean from the unclean.

> *But the Levitical priests, the sons of Zadok, who kept charge of My sanctuary when the sons of Israel went astray from Me, shall come near to Me to minister to Me; and*

they shall stand before Me to offer Me the fat and the blood, declares the Lord God. They shall enter My sanctuary; they shall come near to My table to minister to Me and keep My charge (Ezekiel 44:15-16).

This Zadok priesthood brings an emphasis on the five-fold ministry of inspired teachers as they prepare the Body of Christ to receive the strong apostolic and prophetic ministries yet to commence. These specially anointed saints will provide fresh revelation of God's Word reserved for this generation. Their eyes will be illumined with divine insight and their ears will be opened to the Master teacher's voice. Their emergence will mark a time of transition in leadership for the people of God.

According to Isaiah's commission, when eyes are opened to see and ears are unstopped to hear, then hearts are reconciled to the truth and the people return to the Lord to be healed.

The term "Zadok" is taken from the Hebrew *tzaddik* meaning righteous.[2] It points to the ultimate priesthood of the order of Melchizedek, introduced by the Lord, whom the Scriptures identify as the "king of righteousness" (see Heb. 7). The New Testament considers believers to be part of the priesthood, but a maturing and edifying process is still necessary in order to be molded into the spiritual house the Lord is establishing.

> *You also, as living stones, are being built up as a spiritual house for a holy priesthood, to offer up spiritual sacrifices acceptable to God through Jesus Christ* (1 Peter 2:5).

God's royal government is emerging. It will need to be properly placed in its role as the foundation, with Jesus Christ as chief cornerstone. It will comprise leaders in whom the Lord has found pleasure, who can be trusted with the power and authority necessary for Kingdom purposes to be accomplished in the earth. These emerging leaders are now in a season of pruning and sifting—forging their character to carry this distinct anointing—and are mostly still hidden from wide public view.

They will be judges and counselors ex-employing the sevenfold Spirits of God, who will not judge with their natural eyes nor with their natural ears, but in righteousness make judgments of equity and justice through spiritual discernment (see Isa. 11). The refiner's fire is thoroughly purifying a righteous leadership so the anointing would not be lost nor the wineskins destroyed for lack of character. Such leadership will be a true impartation of the divine nature and holy character established in the spirit and soul of the Lord's government.

INSPIRED PRIESTS

The expression *inspired-priests* is taken from both Old and New Testament Scriptures and generally alludes to teachers who receive their understanding of the Word *"through a revelation of Jesus Christ"* (Gal. 1:12). The apostle Paul stated that his discovery of truth came not by the teaching of man nor by reading a book, but by a divine revelation of Jesus Christ. The inspired priests will present truth that will begin to sanctify believers according to John 17:17, *"Sanctify them in the truth; your word is truth."*

One of the redemptive names of the Lord is Jehovah M'Kaddesh—The Lord Who Sanctifies (see Exod. 31:13). The Hebrew word for "holy" is *Kadosh* and is allied to M'Kaddesh to sanctify, dedicate, consecrate, hallow, or make holy. I Am Jehovah M'Kaddesh—*"the Lord who sanctifies you"* (Exod. 31:13).

In the Old Testament, this term predominantly conveys moral and spiritual purity. In the New Testament, many Scriptures attest to the process of sanctification, accomplished at the cross through the atoning work of Christ. Although our spirit is redeemed with the remission of our sins and acceptance of the Lord, our souls go through a purifying process as we subdue our imaginations and every proud and lofty thing that sets itself against the true knowledge of God. We begin the process of bringing every thought and purpose to the obedience of Christ and His anointing (see 2 Cor. 10:5).

The inspired priests will promote sanctification among believers, making the bride a suitable repository for the fullness of God's Spirit. The *shechinah* of the Bridegroom will empower believers to become partakers of His divine nature and holy character. Inspired priests or teachers are identified with the true biblical definition of discipleship: teaching believers to become the Lord's friends. This form of discipleship will also lead the Body of Christ into the full revelation and realization of the Holy Spirit's fruit mentioned in Galatians 5:22-23.

The main assignment of the inspired teachers will be to biblically reveal the requirements of the Lord for His bride in these latter days to taste the good Word of God and prepare her to walk in the power of the age to come. Through this inspired revelation of the Word by the Holy Spirit, these priests will more fully acquaint believers with the steps of preparation and consecration needed to be viable participants in the glorious ministry yet to come.

CROSSING THE JORDAN

Through Israel we are given types and shadows of our present state. While in Egypt, on the eve of the first Passover, the children of Israel were secure after having applied the blood of the lamb to the doorpost of their dwelling places. Egypt here illustrates the world, and believers are made secure by the application of the Lord's blood to their lives.

Although we remain in the world, we are no longer a part of the world, nor is there contentment of soul while in the land of Egypt. Something new and fresh is now birthed in the heart of believers, causing them to long for the city whose builder and maker is God. Therefore, they leave the "onions and garlic" of the old Egyptian lifestyle and proceed into the wilderness.

Although there may be seasons in which we desire the delicacies of Egypt, our spiritual hunger is for the new corn, olives, wine, figs, and pomegranates of the Promised Land.

Some have visited *Kadesh-Barnea* and ventured over the Jordan into spiritual Canaan and tasted the fruit of that land, but only a few. Instead, on a corporate level, most of us have been intimidated by the giants and walled cities and have refused to possess the land promised as our inheritance.

Time has now come for a company of people to possess the promised rest and dispossess the giants of the soul. The promised land is a spiritual habitation and communion with Christ producing fruitfulness and yielding the same and greater works as He did while on earth in human form...thus fulfilling the prophetic declaration of John 14:12. The Promised Land will be the realization of the Lord's prayer—*"Thy Kingdom come, thy will be done, in earth as it is in Heaven"* (Matt. 6:10 KJV).

CLEANSING THE SOUL

The Lord is looking for men and women who live in agreement with His Word and stand before Him as His spokespeople, who become the expression of His voice. Those God views as overcomers will be granted a white stone and have a new name imparted to them. This place in God allows us to share in the hidden manna reserved for the time of the end. Secrets and mysteries are yet to be unfolded from the depths of God's Word that will transform the bride and make her ready for the Bridegroom.

Therefore, having these promises, beloved, let us cleanse ourselves from all defilement of flesh and spirit, perfecting holiness in the fear of God (2 Corinthians 7:1).

Conversely, there is a demonically inspired "dark light" that will send deluding influences into the souls of many people with delusions of grandeur. That is why we must continually cleanse ourselves from all that would contaminate and defile both body and spirit (see 1 John 1:9). Delusions of grandeur and spiritual deceptions result in the manipulation of the Church body through selfish ambition and self-justification. These will utilize control and religious spirits to accomplish a counterfeit agenda and twist God's Word to suit that agenda.

The Lord's servants are always meek and teachable. The Holy Spirit is beckoning us back to humble hearts and contrite spirits, trembling at the Word of the Lord. Out of this devotion, we will easily discern the demonic influences the enemy tries to initiate in us and quickly dispel them. This process will keep us "hallowed" before the Lord.

This season of the Spirit will emphasize purification and cleansing of the soul. As we submit to this process, we will begin to grow in the things of God and share in His divine nature and holy character. This sacred promise will be released in the Body of Christ through anointed vessels bringing to life the Word of God through demonstrations of the Holy Spirit. They will ascend to heights in God with anointed eyes and ears and report what they have seen and heard and, like John, say:

> *What we have seen and heard we proclaim to you also, so that you too may have fellowship with us; and indeed our fellowship is with the Father, and with His Son Jesus Christ* (1 John 1:3).

ENDNOTES

1.   *Phroureo,* Strong's 5432/Vine's Dictionary.

2.   *Tzaddik,* Strong's 6659/Vine's Dictionary; http://strongsnumbers.com/hebrew/6659.htm.

Chapter 12

SPIRITUAL THOUGHTS AND SPIRITUAL WORDS

Through the Church, the Holy Spirit is beginning to unveil the mysteries of the Kingdom by articulating and giving expression to spiritual thoughts with spiritual words (see 1 Cor. 2:13). It will be Kingdom truth not taught by human wisdom, but the Holy Spirit granting the proper interpretation of spiritual truth through spiritual language. If we choose a receptive posture in this process, we will begin to understand His ways and apprehend His thoughts. The Lord is promising to reveal His thoughts and ways, which are much higher than ours, if we will only follow his prescription for a *higher way* of holiness.

Words, when anointed, become a spiritual vehicle that transports us from one realm to another; or, put another way, the natural word becomes spiritual through the anointing of the Holy Spirit. In John 6:63, Jesus stated the words He spoke to them were both Spirit and life: *"It is the Spirit who gives life; the flesh profits nothing; the words that I have spoken to you are spirit and are life."*

Through the anointing of the Holy Spirit, words attain a spiritual life of their own. The Spirit gives life to the message of the Kingdom, which points to the cross and transports one from the natural into the Spirit realm. At that crossroad, we discover the hope of our calling and the immeasurable greatness of His unlimited power toward those who believe.

Jesus Himself was actually representative of the "anointed Word." He was the Word of God incarnate and He is the Messiah, which translated means the Anointed One. His anointing is the fuel that propels the vehicle. Without the anointing, the vehicle cannot operate. *"The letter kills, but the Spirit gives life"* (2 Cor. 3:6).

For the ministered Word to become spiritual food, it must proceed from the Lord's Presence through an anointed ministry in an atmosphere of the anointing. As His anointed Word is quickened within us and we receive from it an impartation of Spirit and life, we are then growing into His full stature.

Truth Springing Forth From the Earth

Acquiring knowledge about the Bible is a noble pursuit. However, it cannot be a substitute for knowing Jesus intimately as the Living Word. He is living Truth. A *word* is a thought that has been given expression. Inherent in God are His attributes and thoughts. God gave articulation to His thoughts and virtues through the Word (Logos). The *Word* then became flesh and dwelt among us so we could behold His glory and comprehend the perceptions and qualities of God. Truth sprang forth from the very heart of God in Word form, imparting Spirit and life that is tangible spiritual substance.

Surely His salvation is near to those who fear Him that glory may dwell in our land. Lovingkindness and truth have met together; righteousness and peace have kissed each other. Truth springs from the earth; and righteousness looks down from heaven (Psalm 85:9-11).

The Holy Spirit's spotlight will be on Kingdom truths expressed in the above passage. The salvation here promised is not restricted to eternal life in our heavenly home, but includes deliverance of all kinds—rescue from trouble, distress, and calamity in this generation.

All who truly reverence Him and possess the fear of God rather than the fear of man may expect His impressive support and aid! God desires that the people called by His name possess the confident assurance that He will intervene in their troubles and deliver them. It is the heart cry of all God's children to see His glory abiding in the land. As the prophet David once wrote: *"For Thy lovingkindness is before mine eyes, and I have walked in Thy truth"* (Ps. 26:3 KJV).

As we discover the fullness of the Spirit of Truth and walk faithfully, we will experience His promised inheritance set before our eyes. The Kingdom's benefits—God's glory, loving-kindness, mercy, righteousness, and peace—are produced by the Spirit of Truth. If we are going to be fruitful, we must be faithful to the Spirit of Truth.

The Spirit of Truth will expose the spirit of deception. When this is accomplished, great conflict results between the two camps. Again, we are confronted in our choices by the testing of our motives and desires. If we embrace the correct commission, we will be catapulted to greater measures of loving-kindness and righteousness, and we will experience heightened expressions of His glory.

Testing produces choices that we must make in righteousness as we *choose each* day whom we shall serve. We must especially pray for a guard to be placed before our tongues so that our words are spoken in agreement with Him. Our prayerful petition should continually be for awakened spiritual senses and a covering to be placed around our hearts so we will not embrace deceptions—only the Spirit of Truth.

All our words should be galvanized with charity. Even if words of correction are necessary, when vitalized with charity they will always be fruitful because love never fails.

As a result, we are no longer to be children,
tossed here and there by waves, and carried

about by every wind of doctrine, by the trickery of men, by craftiness in deceitful scheming; but speaking the truth in love, we are to grow up in all aspects into Him, who is the head, even Christ (Ephesians 4:14-15).

If we do not cultivate a love for the truth, especially in the season ahead, we will be turned over to a spirit of delusion. The apostle Paul prophetically envisioned this day and wrote of it:

The one whose coming is in accord with the activity of Satan, with all power and signs and false wonders, and with all the deception of wickedness for those who perish, because they did not receive the love of the truth so as to be saved. And for this reason God will send upon them a deluding influence so that they will believe what is false (2 Thessalonians 2:9-11).

Unfortunately, many erroneous doctrines continue to be embraced in the Church, providing veils that separate us from the One we seek. A powerful release of the Spirit of Truth is coming to those of God's people who are endowed with eyes to see and ears to hear.

This visitation of truth is to guide us into all truth, dispelling the lies that have been taught as truth.

ENCOUNTERING THE TEACHER

Our response to our Teacher's voice is the key that opens the door inviting us to *"Come up here, and I will show you what must take place after these things"* (Rev. 4:1). Once we do, we will discover great and mighty things that we presently do not know, through close encounter with the Lord Himself.

> *Although the Lord has given you bread of privation and water of oppression, He, your Teacher will no longer hide Himself, but your eyes will behold your Teacher. Your ears will hear a word behind you, "This is the way, walk in it," whenever you turn to the right or to the left* (Isaiah 30:20-21).

Teachers will emerge who have encountered the Teacher and heard expressions from His lips that will provide clear and concise direction to prevent us from stepping waywardly to the right or left. The path we have been called to travel is straight and narrow. We can only remain on this path if we are being ushered by the Spirit of Truth and embracing every word that proceeds from the mouth of God.

The Scriptures are not a matter of private interpretation, but people moved by the Holy Spirit will speak from God's anointing by what they see and hear. Their message will reveal the mysteries of the Kingdom to prepare the Bride like Esther, to be without spot or wrinkle and marinated in honest and sincere hearts.

Idolatry and human precepts will be put away and dispensed by the Bride as impure when the Living Word makes Himself known. The prophet Isaiah used this metaphor to portray to the nation of Israel as the hideous nature of false teachings and idolatry esteemed by God's people.

Much *gold and silver* have been generated from teachings that have measures of truth but have been taken well beyond their prescribed parameters. This has caused great confusion and disillusionment among many in the Church and has brought a reproach upon God's people from the very ones needing the Gospel. The Lord is announcing His intention to begin dealing with these issues. Truth shall spring forth from the earth through the hearts of God's people, as the Spirit of Truth descends upon the Church.

When the Helper comes, whom I will send to you from the Father, that is the Spirit of truth, who proceeds from the Father, He will testify about Me, and you will testify also, because you have been with Me from the beginning (John 15:26-27).

Mature teachers will be primarily commissioned to direct the people to the truth—Jesus is the Truth. Christ is both the Way and the Truth, and the Holy Spirit is the Guide who shows the way to Him. The Lord desires to be the Teacher for all who believe. Anointed instructors will present to the people the seeds of biblical truth and point the way for everyone to cultivate one's own relationship with the Lord. It is His great pleasure to enlighten His people in the ways of Kingdom life.

REREADING SCRIPTURES WITH SPIRITUAL EYES

A clear injunction is emanating from the Holy Spirit directing us to truly reread the written Word through spiritual eyes. Passages of Scripture we have read many times will begin to take on new life as a fresh dimension of insight is deposited from Heaven's throne. For many passages, it will be as though we have never read them because of the unique hidden truth that will emerge in this day. Even the prophet Daniel foresaw our generation and understood that the revelations he was privileged to observe were reserved for the time of the end. We have now entered that day, and the present dimensions of truth will be unveiled.

> *But when He, the Spirit of Truth, comes, He will guide you into all the truth; for He will not speak on His own initiative, but whatever He hears, He will speak; and He will disclose to you what is to come* (John 16:13).

The influence of this fresh revelation of truth will begin to transform our natures from being waywardly based in fear to securely fashioned in faith. On the surface, this shift will make the coming days seem turbulent. Despite this, the end result will be the reestablishing of the Church on a firm foundation of truth and faith. Fear is a great enemy the Lord desires to overcome in His people. As He did with Joshua of old, God is enjoining us to be strong and of good courage, without fear or reservation in our approach to this next season of the Spirit.

LIVING IN A NEW DAY

With the dawning of this new day in Church history, the anointing of Heaven is being disbursed into the spiritual atmosphere so those seeking truth can lay hold of it and obtain great insight with understanding. As the Lord's people ask with sincerity for this deposit, they will receive it. Our spiritual eyes will be illumined to see the scriptures from Heaven's perspective, not merely those presented through human reasoning.

The spiritual realities being birthed in the earth now will have no end. They will literally flow into the millennial age and the coming manifestation of God's Kingdom on earth. Although we do not know when those days will be fully revealed, we do know that the purposes now being birthed will advance directly into that millennial age.

We will begin to taste the good Word of God and the power of the age to come. Like the beloved disciple John in his notable revelations, we will be allowed to eat the open book containing the full manifestation of the Lord's redemptive plans and purposes. This will be the tasting of His Kingdom word and a demonstration of Kingdom might, in order to wonderfully introduce the Lord Jesus in truth and power to an entire generation.

SPIRITUAL BENEFICIARIES

W hen we engage the revelatory realm of Heaven, it carries us into a supernatural dimension of faith in which miracles, deliverances, signs, and wonders result. The healing expression of the 1940s and 1950s introduced a more pronounced Kingdom ministry from the revelatory realm that opened the Heavens for a season of healing and miracles unprecedented in Church history. During that time, many souls came into the Kingdom and truth was restored.

On May 7, 1946, William Branham went to a secret place of prayer, a cabin tucked deep in the woods of Indiana. This godly man had been experiencing supernatural encounters for which neither he nor his fellow ministers had a grid or base of understanding to compare.

Finally, in desperation, he retreated to this secluded place, determined to discover from the Lord what these things were and their significance.

According to his testimony, something supernatural occurred well into the night and deep into his heartfelt time of prayer—a heavenly light entered the room in which he was praying. The supernatural light appeared as a pillar of fire and projected illumination in much the same way that a spotlight would. At that moment he heard footsteps walking toward him and eventually standing under the beam of light. One can only imagine the frightful reaction of someone alone, deep in a wooded area without electricity and encountering a supernatural being walking into the room in a real and tangible way.

The angelic messenger's audible salutation was similar to those we discover in the Scriptures. He said, "Fear not, for I am sent from the Presence of Almighty God." As soon as Branham heard this voice, he recognized it as the one who had spoken to him many times throughout his life. The messenger continued by saying that he was sent to impart a commission of divine healing to that generation.

However, an additional, unique aspect of the commission introduced a fresh dimension of the revelatory realm of Heaven, which accompanied Branham's already tremendous healing ministry. A supernatural gift was imparted to allow this man to detect by revelation the specific illnesses, demonic oppressions, and deadly diseases afflicting people. He was further instructed that if he walked humbly in this gift, he would at some point be allowed to discern the very thoughts and intents of the heart.

This commissioning introduced a more amplified expression of the omniscient attributes of the Lord than had previously been known in that era. When God released this supernatural revelation, the people's faith soared above the realm of doubt and unbelief into the realm of faith where miracles are accessed.[1]

On June 14, 1946, the first public healing meeting under this commissioning took place in St. Louis, Missouri. The impact and responses were immediate. Miracles began to occur on a mass scale, and many writers of that day determined that the number was unprecedented in modern Church history.

When the Lord executed the second phase of the commission, the minister would stand before the people and communicate by revelation their name, illness, resident address, past events, private prayers, and many other detailed secrets that no one knew except them and the Lord. Witnesses testify that this produced such tangible faith in the corporate meetings that the sense prevailed that anything was possible in such an atmosphere of the anointing.[2]

IMPLICATIONS FOR OUR DAY

With something of that magnitude occurring in just the prior generation, we might be compelled to ask the question: What is the significance of this type of ministry for our generation? I believe that this form of ministry was a pioneering work of the Holy Spirit to introduce to our generation the fashion in which the revelatory realm of Heaven can be accessed to release supernatural faith. William Branham's was a forerunner ministry.

The events occurring between 1946 and 1956 were much more than just a revival. They were the beginning of the end-time ministry that initiated the fulfillment of prophetic Scriptures pointing to this generation. As with Moses, these signs were given so that the people would believe:

> *And it shall come to pass, if they will not believe thee, neither hearken to the voice of the first sign, that they will believe the voice of the latter sign* (Exodus 4:8 KJV).

According to the commission given to Moses, these supernatural signs have a voice. There is a message accompanying the signs. The message is one of restoration of God's covenant people to a place of spiritual prominence and submission to the Messiah's lordship. The message was much more than a gift of the Spirit; it was the manifestation of the Person of the Word discerning the thoughts and intents of the heart.

> *For the word of God is living and active, and sharper than any two-edged sword, and piercing as far as the division of soul and spirit, of both joints and marrow, and able to judge the thoughts and intentions of the heart. And there is no creature hidden from His sight, but all things are open and laid bare to the eyes of Him with whom we have to do* (Hebrews 4:12-13).

The Living Word discerns and peers directly into the secret corridors of our lives. All things are open and laid bare before the eyes of Him with whom we have to do. When the Spirit of the Lord manifests in a tangible way, it brings forth revelation, not merely as a *word of knowledge* but as the Spirit of Knowledge and Revelation flowing to benefit God's people. It carries the reassuring virtue that God not only knows about us individually but cares and is willing to give expression to the understanding of His heart.

AWAKENING SPIRITUAL DESTINY

The Lord Jesus Himself used this aspect of His virtue in His encounter with the woman at the well (see John 4). What an incredible privilege was given to this precious woman who received a private audience with the Son of God. Jesus dismissed His disciples and waited for this woman to come to the well because He knew that resident inside her was a seed of destiny that only needed light from Heaven to envelope it with faith and purpose.

In a unique way, the Lord chose to engage the revelatory realm of Heaven to awaken this woman to her destiny, rather than display a demonstration of

His great power. Clearly, He could have performed a notable miracle or allowed her to witness the restoration of blind eyes or lame limbs. Instead, He chose to disclose to her the secrets of her heart and share lovingly all that she had ever done. He related personal insight about her life that she knew He had no way of knowing through natural means.

Jesus did this because He knew that a seed of destiny was imparted to her before the foundation of the world; this seed of destiny was looking for a promised Messiah. Her response points to this reality:

> *I know that Messiah is coming (He who is called Christ); when that One comes, He will declare all things to us. Jesus said to her, "I who speak to you am He"* (John 4:25-26).

Through this encounter, insight was shared from the revelatory realm of Heaven inflaming her supernatural faith. She now possessed the capacity to believe for the restoration and revival of her city. Oblivious to the obvious shame she must have carried from a history of failure that included a current relationship that was not lawful and five prior husbands, she returned to her fellow Samaritans with a message of hope and expectancy.

Her faith ignited a revival throughout the city; many leaders acknowledged they believed because of her faith, but later they saw for themselves and believed likewise. This is a pattern for harvest set by the Lord that will be used in our generation. Jesus employed this occasion to teach His followers a model for spiritual harvest. The fields are white for harvest and awaiting the anointed laborers. He has made provision for us in this hour to be anointed in like fashion. What an incredible redemptive promise!

THE SPIRIT OF THE LORD IS UPON ME

The commission God desires to impart to this generation we find in Luke 4:18. The Spirit of the Lord coming upon a consecrated and prepared body of people to release—counsel and might; wisdom and revelation; knowledge and the reverential fear of God.

> *The Spirit of the Lord is upon Me, because He anointed Me to preach the gospel to the poor. He has sent Me to proclaim release to the captives, and recovery of sight to the*

blind, to set free those who are oppressed,
to proclaim the favorable year of the Lord
(Luke 4:18-19).

That is the Kingdom reality that rested upon the Lord Jesus and the one that was restored in 1946. It is far more than ministry or the exercise of spiritual gifts. It is His divine Presence. It is the Spirit of the Lord overshadowing His Bride and inciting her to do the same works He did while on earth in human form.

The greatest gift is to be able to step aside so He can step in and do through us the same works He did. That is what was introduced to us through the prior generation and the incredible demonstration of Kingdom power and authority witnessed in that day. A few touched that realm as spiritual spies who introduced it to the present generation of destiny.

Many ministers from the prior generation, who flowed in realms of power as healing evangelists, were devoted and sincere saints of God. They initially approached the Lord in simplicity and humility and obtained from Him the anointing needed to carry the gospel of salvation and power to an entire generation. Even so, the prior generation did not enter into the fullness of the promise nor sustain the unveiling of the Kingdom message. If that can happen to them, how much more to us in this day! We need God's great grace to access and sustain the open Heaven needed to fulfill the harvest generation.

Such was Joshua's commission:

> *Moses My servant is dead; now therefore arise, cross this Jordan, you and all this people, to the land which I am giving to them, to the sons of Israel...No man will be able to stand before you all the days of your life. Just as I have been with Moses, I will be with you; I will not fail you or forsake you* (Joshua 1:2,5).

Although Joshua was anointed with the same Spirit that rested upon Moses, his ministry to the people had little similarity in its application. There was no need for Joshua to write the law; that was already accomplished by Moses. The Spirit that had rested on Moses and was imparted to Joshua unveiled another aspect of the Lord as the Warrior who displaced the giants usurping a place in the land promised to God's covenant people.

The scribe of the Kingdom brings forth from his treasure things old and new. While we examine the prior expression of God's magnificent manifested Presence, we must also remain open to the unprecedented demonstrations of the Spirit. Eye has not seen and ear has not heard nor has it yet entered into the heart of man all that will be revealed through the mind of Christ in this day. We only know it will be tremendous and require eyes and ears opened to the revelatory realm of Heaven and a wholly submitted spirit, soul, and body.

ENDNOTES

1.   My conclusions are derived from listening to hundreds of the messages preached by William Branham and testimony from numerous eye witnesses.

2.   Ibid.

About the Author

Paul Keith Davis spent 20 years in the business arena before entering full-time ministry. He and his wife, Wanda, founded WhiteDove Ministries after the Lord sovereignly sent a beautiful white dove to them as a prophetic sign of their calling. In recent years, they have traveled extensively speaking at conferences and churches imparting the end-time mandate of preparation for the glory and manifest presence of Christ.

Paul Keith has written numerous articles for various Christian publications, including the *MorningStar Journal* and Church Growth International. For the past several years, he has also co-written with Bob Jones *The Shepherd's Rod*, which provides spiritual insight.

His first book, *The Thrones of Our Soul*, was written as a clarion call to the end-time generation.

His heart's desire is to see the full restoration of biblical apostolic ministry manifested through the Spirit of Truth that brings salvation, healing, and deliverance. He has a unique gift for imparting prophetic understanding regarding the times and seasons and declaring a message of preparation and expectancy for the Lord's empowering presence.

Paul Keith and his wife, Wanda, reside in Orange Beach, Alabama. Together, they have five children and three grandchildren.

Also by
PAUL KEITH DAVIS

Thrones Of Our Souls:
Prophetic Mandates For The
End-Time Generation

With great spiritual insight, Paul Keith
Davis explains how God deals with
the sacred places that keep us from
achieving our prophetic destiny. Join
Paul Keith on an inspiring journey
into God's heart for your life.

Order online at
www.whitedoveministries.org

Additional copies of this book and other
book titles from DESTINY IMAGE are
available at your local bookstore.

Call toll-free: 1-800-722-6774.

Send a request for a catalog to:

Destiny Image® Publishers, Inc.

P.O. Box 310
Shippensburg, PA 17257-0310

*"Speaking to the Purposes of God for This
Generation and for the Generations to Come."*

**For a complete list of our titles,
visit us at www.destinyimage.com.**